J ERIC WILSON and
R JUSTEN COLLINS

𝔚e
𝔖urround
𝔗hem

Our Journey from Apathy to Action

Basil,
Thanks For everything
you Do. keep Active

Justen
BDC
Collins

ISBN: 0615446752
ISBN-13: 9780615446752

Contents

Foreword

The 9/12 Project kicked off in March of 2009. Americans had become increasingly disillusioned with the direction of their beloved country. For years, we had watched our government implementing their socialistic agenda, recklessly spending our money, and ignoring the law of the land - our Constitution. While we recognized that this had been taking place for many years, what had long been a slow march toward a socialist takeover of the country was now entering a full-on sprint under our new president's agenda.

Although bewildered at first, we were reminded - through this project's inception - of who we were as Americans on September 12, 2001, the day after the worst attack on American soil. We stood shoulder-to-shoulder with our fellow countrymen, unconcerned about our different religious beliefs, different skin colors, or different political parties. We remembered who we are as Americans - the people who made this the greatest country in the world. We recognized that we needed to stand together again, rise up to defend our Constitution, and dedicate ourselves to living life in accordance with the Principles and Values we all shared.

Soon, tens of thousands of people began logging onto the 9/12 Project website searching for a group in their area. Several individuals, including myself, worked overtime trying to connect people to groups forming near them. Due to the overwhelming amount of inquiries, willing individuals were identified in many states to help expedite the process. Eric Wilson from Kentucky was one of those individuals.

As The 9/12 Project was forming, we were charged with reconnecting with our communities. Get to know your neighbors, start around your kitchen tables, educate yourself on what our Founding Fathers intended for our country. Many people felt that this was a "calling" so to speak, and they had to get personally involved. Something had been missing in their lives, but they had never before been able put their finger on it.

My expertise on volunteer-based organizations provides me with the background and firsthand knowledge of this process typically works. Social movements - as well as the members within them - can head in many directions, as you will read in this book. People, with the best of intentions, sign up with local organizations only to have second thoughts once the commitment is made. People volunteer because their heart tells them they need to give back to their communities. Soon, though, the doubts of what they have just gotten involved in start to take over. They wonder if they will have the time to spare in addition to family, work, and other obligations.

In Eric's case, he and his wife had just had a baby. That is precisely what motivated him and the other members of the Kentucky 9/12 group. We need to do this for our children in order to provide them with a base of principles and values and an education on what America is all about. If we don't do it, then who will? I first spoke with Eric in May of 2009 and ever since that time, he has been one of the most dedicated, understanding, and motivated volunteers in our movement.

During this period, a march was being organized to be held in Washington, D.C. on September 12, 2009. Once The 9/12 Project made the decision to participate, a call went out to all of our members. Shortly afterward, Eric informed me that the Kentucky 9/12 group was putting together a separate event in D.C. before the march for all interested 9/12ers to attend. As a great example of how the Kentucky group operates, they took full responsibility for running the event. They had an idea, went to work, and got it done! They didn't sit around and wait for someone to give them directions. That is exactly the intent of The 9/12 Project and the true spirit of "We the People!" Being Constitutionalists, we strongly believe in governing ourselves, not waiting for the government or any organization to tell us what needs to be done.

I had no idea what to expect at the event in Washington. It was simply amazing! The event was filled with enthusiasm and joy, but what really struck me was the people that I met. We laughed and cried together that night, and now two years later, I can proudly say I call many of those individuals my true friends.

I believe that - as a whole - 9/12ers are people who walk the walk. Before the project was ever even a thought, we were the people who led our lives by the Principles and Values that our parents and grandparents taught us. Though certainly not perfect, we strive to work at demonstrating those qualities so that we will hopefully be examples for others in our communities.

People around the country have story after story of the friendships they have made through their 9/12 groups. I hear the stories as groups move through the stages that all social movements experience - groups moving in a direction that not everyone is comfortable with or always having to rely on the same individuals volunteering to get things done – the typical growing pains that are the important part of development. But the consistent theme that runs through everyone's stories is the relationships that have been built from participating in The 9/12 Project. That, my friends, is what it is all about!

What makes us unique is our set of beliefs, our dedication to educating ourselves, our communities, and our children about our Constitution, our Founding Fathers' original intent, and an understanding of the processes of our government. The 9/12 Project will be around for many years. We will never run out of ideas as to how to educate ourselves. Not as long as groups like KY9/12 exist, not as long as people like yourself stay standing, and most importantly, not as long as we all remain true to our Principles and Values.

Yvonne Donnelly
National Director - The 9/12 Project
January 2011

Learn more and become involved at www.the912project.com

Introduction

Imagine I told you to go out and find 150 complete strangers willing to assemble themselves at a local pizza place one weekday evening to watch an hour of cable television together.

It is a strange request, I know. The thought probably conjures up images of a large room filled with hushed attempts at awkward conversations. The human curiosity that would be needed to draw a crowd is slowly replaced by anxiety as people begin to size each other up and wonder what potential impact their decision to attend could have upon them.

Now imagine that, instead of quiet and uncomfortable, this room of complete strangers is instead welcoming and engaging to those that enter it. Imagine that the awkward interactions that you anticipated are replaced by the sounds of lasting relationships being formed as people exchange names and contact information with one another. Imagine the group decides this will not be a one-time assembly, and they begin to make plans to get back together in the coming weeks.

If your imagination is still with me at this point, let's take it one step further. Imagine that, out of this gathering of strangers, a core group of like-minded individuals emerges with a desire to work together for a common cause. Imagine that within twenty months this core group evolves into an active non-profit corporation and receives international attention in the process.

I suppose it takes a pretty active imagination to envision this particular chain of social events. What could possibly drive a crowd of strangers gathered in front of a television at a local pizza joint to begin to volunteer their time and energy for a group that did not even exist the day before? How could that group — regardless of its dedication — make an impact on its community in such a short period of time?

The story of the Kentucky 9/12 Project goes from pizza to politics and from Kentucky to Washington, D.C. and back a few times. It is a story about a group struggling to find its identity and making plenty of wrong turns along the way. Most of all, it is a story about an amazing group of talented and dedicated individuals coming together and selflessly using their time and abilities for a common cause. Those personal sacrifices served to inspire thousands across their state, but the impact of their actions and ideas resonated around the entire country.

My name is Eric Wilson, and I am the Executive Director of the Kentucky 9/12 Project. I was lucky enough to be along for the entire ride and to meet all of these wonderful people, and I hope that sharing these stories pays proper tribute to the events and to those individuals. The "imaginary" scenario that I have just outlined for you is actually our true story, and it all began with a frustrated caller to a talk radio program.

Unrest

(noun) an uneasy or troubled state.

Genesis

January 27, 2009 began for me in much the same fashion as any other day at the office. That morning, I was sitting at my desk and mindlessly scanning across the AM dial. My routine had become predictable most days, and the radio served as a welcome distraction from the office sounds around me. I eventually settled in on my preferred background noise of talk radio. I was hardly paying attention at all until something caught my ear midway through the Glenn Beck program when he took an interesting call from a listener.

GLENN: Let me go to Ed in New Haven listening to us on WELI. Hi, Ed!
CALLER: Glenn, no matter how this call ends, I just want you to know that I respect you more than anybody out there in the news media.
GLENN: Oh, boy.
CALLER: You changed my life in a positive way and I think in God's eyes that's one of the only things that really you can do.
GLENN: Wow, thank you very much.
CALLER: However, however.
GLENN: Yes.
CALLER: You got a letter yesterday or something about somebody saying they're going to tune out?
GLENN: Yes. They said that they were going to unplug because they felt too small, too insignificant and they couldn't make any difference and they were just getting angry and frustrated. So they were done.

I am not sure if it was the tone of the caller or just the mood I was in, but somehow I was already connecting to this conversation. Whatever the reason, I stopped working and began to listen closer now.

CALLER: I thought I would call in and give my perspective if anyone was really interested in it because it's very amazing the feelings that I'm getting from doing this - of guilt and also a feeling of half of me says I'm doing the right thing and the other half of me is really making me feel really guilty about it. The gamut of emotions: it's really a weird feeling.

GLENN: I gave up television and that included all - this was during the Monica Lewinsky thing - all television news and everything and I just read the newspaper and kept to speed like that, and it was a wild experiment, absolutely wild. Changed my life, changed my attitude. But I understand what you're saying about guilt. Let me - may I heap a little guilt on you?

CALLER: Sure.

GLENN: Quote from James Madison:"A well-instructed people alone can be permanently a free people." Another one from Thomas Jefferson:"If a nation expects to be ignorant and free, in a state of civilization, it expects what never was and never will be." The unfortunate thing, Ed, is I really truly believe that is part of the design to get you to tune out, to get you to stop watching, to get you to stop paying attention, to get you to the point of frustration to where you throw up your hands and say, "I can't really even care anymore. I'm just going to conduct my own life." Because when you do that, then they have control over you because no one is standing guard anymore.

CALLER: Well, I understand that, but I think you ought to know one other thing.

GLENN: Yes.

CALLER: I really tuned out. Not a magazine, not a paper, nothing. I mean nothing. The only thing I had in the background is you and Rush as background music for major headlines. I didn't even know we went - Israel, you know, was tossing bombs around with the Palestinians. I knew nothing about that until one day I saw a headline when I went to buy some gum. I really tuned out, I think, a little bit more than you think and -

GLENN: *Oh, no, you just tuned out as much as most people do in America. They just, they get their news from Jon Stewart and watch American Idol. That's what most people do.*

CALLER: *You are right. I'm one of the zombies that I complained about for twenty years and I'm one of them now, but I can't bring myself back. Every time I try to turn the TV on and take a look...I'm like, you know what, click. I went right back again. You know?*

GLENN: *Okay, here's - Ed, I completely understand and this is something that I - in fact, I just said the other day...*

By this point, my full attention was focused in on the radio. I related to everything Ed from Connecticut was saying, and I was hanging on every answer Glenn provided. I could see that my wife and I had begun to tune out lately as well. We were becoming those zombies watching reality TV as an escape from the true reality happening in our country. What could we do, though? Was there really any hope for a solution? I listened on, hoping to find that answer.

GLENN: *Freedom is a very delicate thing and if you are not standing guard, well, then you are truly not honoring the people. Was it easier to land on Omaha Beach, was it easier to leave your home, watch it be burned to the ground during the Revolutionary War? Was it easier for those people to do those things? The answer is no. We're saying we don't even want to watch the news because we're frustrated. We just want to go back to our life. We are dishonoring those who went before us who actually died for this freedom that we now just say I want to unplug from.*

CALLER: *Yeah, but there's more going on, Glenn. My heart goes out to those people. Believe me, I cry just at the sight of those monuments and the thought of what those people did for me. The problem is* *today - and I believe this. I believe that we're outnumbered now. I don't believe -*

GLENN:*We're not. We're not.*

CALLER:*I know you say that, and I knew you were going to get mad at me.*

GLENN:*We're not, damn it!*

CALLER:*I knew it.*

GLENN:*We're not outnumbered. We're not outnumbered.*

CALLER:*You look at the polls. Every -*

GLENN:*You know what, I - here's the thing. Ed, you give me a month to prove this. I am going to find a way to prove this to you. You know what, Stu, I'm going to - I'm going to give you - Ed, you hang on the phone. I want to get a phone number from you, okay? Thank you for calling. And Ed, you are the probably - you could be the most important caller that I have ever received in my career.*

Like many others around the nation, I sat in silence as Ed hung up the phone and Glenn continued with his monologue. Among the first thoughts that came to my mind were that if anyone had the right to give up, it was not Ed or myself but the many others that had warned of the approaching iceberg for years only to see their warnings go unheeded. Did I have any right to give up or give in now?

As I listened, I shared the feelings of despair that I had just heard Ed describe, and I also shared his sense of isolation from what I perceived to be the majority of Americans. Now, Glenn Beck had accepted the challenge of proving that we were not alone and that - in reality - there were more of us than the elitist political class we felt overwhelmed by. I was willing to take this ride and anxious to see where the journey would take us, but it was going to take serious convincing for me to shake those initial feelings of uneasiness.

I now realize that all social movements are rooted in some unease. For some, it is a feeling of isolation and powerlessness. For others, it is frustration and being dissatisfied with current affairs. For me and thousands of other Americans, the phone call from Ed in Connecticut proved to be a conversation that personalized and amplified our uneasiness about the state of our nation. While the spirit, principles, and values that would soon come together to form the 9/12 Project movement had been alive and growing in others for decades, this phone call became a rallying cry and turning point for many more. Of course, I pay the deepest respect to the people and patriots that have been aware and fighting the fight for years, but I found myself in a new group of people that were awakened at last by Ed's call. Though we may have been later in arriving to the party, our numbers were growing by the thousands nearly every day.

Over the course of the following weeks, months, and years, we found out that our feelings of unrest were common ground for a diverse group of people. We found the makings of a movement filled with patriots that shared mutual values and beliefs. We found out that we were not surrounded by people who had lost faith in our founding principles and our Constitution.

No, they do not surround us.

We surround them.

~

PRELUDE TO OUR JOURNEY

I am not ashamed to say that my family is possibly the quintessential average Midwest American family. After marrying my wife, Lydia, we decided to relocate in order to be closer to the church we wanted to attend. As soon as I found a new job, we gave up the rolling cornfields of Ohio for the rolling horse pastures of central Kentucky. We bought a nice average-sized home in a large "cookie cutter" subdivision full of similar houses on postage stamp-sized grass lots. In no time at all, Lydia had taken the house from being just a new place to hang our hats and transformed it into our "home sweet home."

As 2009 began, we had two pre-teen children, Aaron and Sarah, and an unexpected-but-welcome new baby just a few months away. Lydia was the stay-at-home mom who kept our home and family running through her work as the wife, mother, and caretaker for everything. Financially, we were much like any other middle class family in America. We made ends meet without major stress, but we would forgo vacations and certain luxuries quite often to give our kids a little more. I spent days at work and evenings on the couch with my lovely wife watching television. Add to that mix a cat with no tail, and you have our ordinary days and generally serene lifestyle.

I can't completely say I was politically unaware and uninterested prior to the 9/12 Project movement. I can say - knowing what I know now - that I was politically and historically ignorant, and the more I learn, the more I realize I still don't know. I had previously been active in occasionally campaigning for local candidates and by serving on the County Republican Party Central Committee when I lived in Ohio. My most extensive participation came during the 2004 Bush re-election campaign where I was the county team leader for a 72-hour pre-election task force. I was also one of the "evil poll watchers" made infamous while observing for any signs of voter fraud during that election.

Politics, though, to me had always been a spectator sport and one that I honestly enjoyed to watch. I would compare election night coverage to my personal Super Bowl, as I would stay up and anxiously watch results. Those results rarely meant anything personal to me, though, and the implications were only superficial when my "side" won or lost.

It was with the election of 2008 that for the first time my eyes began to open that I no longer had a "side." It was hearing people like Glenn Beck and reading books like "The 5000 Year Leap" that smacked me upside the head and revealed that elections truly had consequences. It was early in the new presidential administration that I began to see those consequences, and I feared for our country.

Lydia had been even less politically active in her past, but she was equally aware of national events. While I had been an avid listener of talk radio for over a decade, my wife was not a fan. When we first got to know one another, she laughed when I told her about my listening habits. After we were married, I managed to introduce her to Rush Limbaugh's radio show, and she quickly became a "ditto head" and "Rush babe." I guess Rush just has that effect on the ladies! Soon, I would come home to find her listening to talk radio, watching Fox News, and surfing the internet for articles on politics and current events.

All these sources of information represented quite a change from the influences Lydia had experienced in prior years. She had been employed in social work and daily found herself surrounded by left-of-center ideology. There was abundant encouragement to support Democrats on the perceived notion that this would make it easier to maintain their funding and their jobs.

I believe September 11, 2001 and the horrific attack on our country was perhaps the first moment where Lydia's thinking began to shift. As time progressed and the war on terror raged on, raising a new son led her to consider the safety and security of our country, and she became ideologically conservative in her attitude toward our nation's handling of terrorism. Soon, she began to see things differently in regards to her own profession as well. As a believer in personal responsibility, she struggled with the special treatment people would sometimes receive in response to misfortunes brought on by their own choices. She saw other areas of social work where the government solutions to problems were becoming an enabling crutch for some.

In time, she became one of the few "closet conservatives" in the social work field, at least until her cover was blown. While I was working on the 2004 Bush campaign, she took a day off from work and attended a rally. All would have been fine, but she ended up being interviewed on national television while holding a "Women for Bush" sign. The next day at work, her secret was out, but it actually turned into a good thing. She found out there were others in her office that shared her views, but they had been afraid to discuss them openly until seeing the interview on the news.

My wife was, is, and always will be a very independent thinker that arrives at her own conclusions. After being introduced to the same media, sharing our experiences with one another, and now witnessing the power grab of our federal government together, she was coming to the same conclusion as me: the things going on in our country were not right. That was the conclusion we came to together toward the end of 2008. This conclusion became the nagging call to action that would prove too strong to resist. It would take an average American couple from sitting in frustration on their couch to being actively involved in restoring our republic. The form that action would eventually take would start to present itself in the first few months of 2009.

∾

JANUARY 2009

As a new year began, my wife and I shared common feelings of concern for our country and worries for its future. Thinking back, the words I remember hearing most from Lydia were "can't anybody else see what is going on?" We saw the policies that were being jammed through our federal government and had the feeling in our guts that something wasn't right. A large part of that feeling was that our individual liberties were under attack. This was about more than policies, and it felt like an attack on our personal values. We were opposed to the government bailouts of private industries, but the media was telling us another story. The story we were being told was that we could not afford to deny these unaffordable bailouts. We were told that these unprecedented times required unprecedented actions even if they were against our country's foundational principles. We were told that it would be far worse if we did nothing.

These media reports sounded more like the propaganda of Bernays than the journalism of Cronkite, but their sales pitches managed to convince some Americans. Those distressed companies were much too big to fail, right? If they were left to collapse, it would tear down the whole economic system, right? Our only salvation was the government. They were the solution, right? Lydia and I were not convinced. Our skepticism for the very political process and politicians we had once observed like a spectator sport reached new heights. We knew in our souls that the immortal words of Ronald Reagan rang equally true today.

"Government is not a solution to our problem, government is the problem."

For the first time in my life, as much as the media tried to convince me of "too big to fail," I arrived at my own conclusion that *nothing* was too big to fail...including our great nation. What an amazing realization: that the country you love - and republic for which you stand - can fall! It was beginning to feel like everything I had been told all my life was now uncertain. There were feelings of fear, feelings of insecurity, and feelings of anger. I now believed we had been deceived for so long, that the only option left for our political establishment was to try to cover up those lies by piling on more and more lies.

Lydia and I were left feeling powerless and alone. We listened to the media and thought we were the only ones that felt this growing frustration. What happened to our country and our principles? What happened to our voice?

Our only bastion of hope was talk radio. While tuning into Glenn Beck, Rush Limbaugh, and a local conservative radio host named Leland Conway, we would hear our own words echoed from the hosts and the people calling into the shows. Yet even there, we felt in the minority and that we were surrounded by those that had the power and set the national agenda.

On January 27, 2009, I was listening to the Glenn Beck radio program. Just as I too was starting to tune out, Ed from Connecticut called in and said most everything I had been thinking. As their conversation unfolded, I leaned my head forward, turned the radio up slightly, stopped everything I was doing, and listened intently through the phone call. My thoughts the entire time was "Yes! Now, what is the solution? What is the answer?" The only response we got was "give me a month, and I will prove that you are not alone." I did not feel any better, but I did have a feeling that Glenn Beck understood. To be honest, though, at this point, trust did not come easy. I had blindly trusted my government my entire life, and we could now see how that worked out for us!

&

FEBRUARY 2009

Maybe I was listening with a new set of ears or maybe tensions were building, but the echoes of my opinions were getting louder and louder and more frequent. Sometimes all it takes is a renewed level of attention to realize that your individual point of view is not unique. It seemed that as we tuned into the news or listened to the radio, more and more often we heard others saying what we were thinking and sharing our building frustration with what was happening in Washington.

In central Kentucky, we had a conservative voice in Leland Conway, a local radio personality that was echoing our uneasiness. The Kentucky 9/12 Project and I owe a debt of gratitude to Leland and his radio show for helping to launch our movement. His show served as an open forum for listeners to connect, and realize that – even in our local area – we were not alone in our feelings. It was one of his radio gimmicks that helped put us over the top and into action. Frustrated at New York Senator Chuck Schumer's statement that people don't care about "pork," he responded by asking listeners to send in bags of pork rinds to be delivered to the Senator's office.

Lydia and I were listening to Leland Conway's show regularly during the early months of 2009, and I remember her reminding me almost daily that we needed to do our part and get some pork rinds to the radio station. A simple act that took only a few dollars from our pockets and minutes of our time served as our introduction to social action. The donation of pork rinds was a small first step, but the national attention it garnered helped us come to the conclusion that we needed to keep active in this budding movement.

LELAND CONWAY

Every radio market has a local voice of conservatism that creates a dedicated following of listeners on the dial. In central Kentucky, we have Leland Conway as that voice who uses the power of the microphone to say many of the things we each wish we could say. A dynamic speaker and show host, Leland's career in radio and television broadcasting spans more than a decade. As listener frustrations built concerning out-of-control government spending and politicians not listening, Leland spoke out. Most notable was the clear and unique message he sent New York Senator Chuck Schumer in the form of 1,500 bags of pork rinds donated by listeners like myself. I guess that is what Chuck deserved after saying "the American people really don't care" about pork! The pork rind delivery received national attention and demonstrated the impact Leland and his show could have, but I am still not convinced even he realizes the influence that he wields. Leland never looks at himself as a leader or mouthpiece for the liberty movement. Instead, he has always been one of us - a proud 9/12er - and he simply speaks from his heart. Outside his work on WLAP 630AM in Lexington, Kentucky, he is not only the founder and executive editor of conservativeedge.com, but there is rarely a tea party, rally, or liberty event in our area that he has not in some way contributed toward.

If we needed another call to action, another one arrived to us in that very same month. In a moment of unscripted exasperation, a CNBC network reporter named Rick Santelli unleashed a live televised tirade against the government's mortgage bailout plans while standing on the floor of the Chicago Mercantile Exchange. Within hours, clips of the broadcast were flying around the internet, and we had yet another reassurance that we were not alone in our assessment of the state of affairs in our federal government.

I watched the video of Santelli's rant online and found myself fascinated by not only the remarks that he made, but also the cheers and applause that he received from the traders that gathered around him as he spoke. It was incredible to see someone passionately expressing the same misgivings that I had about this newest government attempt at economic stimulus and being cheered in the process. One portion of Rick's rant in particular caught my attention as he said, "Cuba used to have mansions and a relatively decent economy. They moved from the individual to the collective. Now they're driving '54 Chevys, maybe the last great car to come out of Detroit. We're thinking of having a Chicago Tea Party in July. All you capitalists that want to show up at Lake Michigan, I'm going to start organizing." This viral video would serve as undeniable proof to a host of Americans like me that our concerns were legitimate and shared by many others.

These increasing signs of ordinary citizens' discontent were all the beginning of a paradigm shift. A social movement was coming together, yet the vast majority of the people involved did not even realize it at the time. Each one was part of the foundation that was being poured and our future was being refined by tools from both sides. On one side we had more and more policies, spending, and larger over-reaching government intrusions building frustration and pushing us away from the founding principles of this nation. On the other side, we had a spontaneous uprising of patriots making a stand and a statement, building passion that something should be done and pushing the nation back to the founding principles.

We were all discovering that there were far more people that shared our personal values than we had ever stopped to imagine. The very belief that Glenn Beck had tried to convey to Ed from Connecticut and had since set out to prove was slowly hitting home with us. Maybe there were others out there that saw what was happening? Maybe we were not alone? Maybe there was still hope? Maybe the Glenn Becks, Leland Conway's, and Rick Santelli's of the world knew what they were talking about? Maybe instead of being hopelessly outnumbered, we literally did surround the vocal minority that was seeking to fundamentally transform our country?

Thankfully, these questions gnawing at our minds would soon become a little easier to answer. We would have an opportunity to identify our like-minded neighbors and unite under a common banner. On the February 9, 2009 episode of Glenn Beck's television show, he laid out a list of principles and values that would come to define our movement:

The Nine Principles

1. America Is Good.

"Love your neighbor as yourself and your country more than yourself." - Thomas Jefferson

2. I believe in God and He is the Center of my Life.

"The propitious smiles of Heaven can never be expected on a nation that disregards the eternal rules of order and right which Heaven itself has ordained." - George Washington

3. I must always try to be a more honest person than I was yesterday.

"I hope that I shall always possess firmness and virtue enough to maintain what I consider to be the most enviable of all titles, the character of an honest man." - George Washington

4. The family is sacred. My spouse and I are the ultimate authority, not the government.

"It is in the love of one's family only that heartfelt happiness is known. By a law of our nature, we cannot be happy without the endearing connections of a family." - Thomas Jefferson

5. If you break the law you pay the penalty. Justice is blind and no one is above it.

"I deem one of the essential principles of our government… equal and exact justice to all men of whatever state or persuasion, religious or political." - Thomas Jefferson

6. I have a right to life, liberty and pursuit of happiness, but there is no guarantee of equal results.

"Everyone has a natural right to choose that vocation in life which he thinks most likely to give him comfortable subsistence." - Thomas Jefferson

7. I work hard for what I have and I will share it with who I want to. Government cannot force me to be charitable.

"It is not everyone who asketh that deserveth charity; all however, are worth of the inquiry or the deserving may suffer." - George Washington

8. It is not un-American for me to disagree with authority or to share my personal opinion.

"In a free and republican government, you cannot restrain the voice of the multitude; every man will speak as he thinks, or more properly without thinking." - George Washington

9. The government works for me. I do not answer to them, they answer to me.
"I consider the people who constitute a society or a nation as the source of all authority in that nation." - Thomas Jefferson

The Twelve Values

1. **Honesty**
2. **Reverence**
3. **Hope**
4. **Thrift**
5. **Humility**
6. **Charity**
7. **Sincerity**
8. **Moderation**
9. **Hard Work**
10. **Courage**
11. **Personal Responsibility**
12. **Gratitude**

Every successful movement has a collective identity that runs in the veins of everyone involved. So many times, those common beliefs go unspoken, but they are still both the foundation upon which everyone builds and the soul of the movement. For us, it was now clearly spelled out and we had a common set of principles and values we could all relate to, reflect on, and respond with in any circumstance.

At least for me, for far too long I had been playing politics and saw the answer to fixing problems in just finding a different politician. In reality, the answer was never politics but principles. Now, the statement of beliefs that Glenn had put together spoke to the heart of what we needed next.

This is why The 9/12 Project is different from the tea party or anything else. This is what separated it from any of the political motivations I may have ever had in the past. Not to disparage anyone else or to say other groups are unprincipled, but I had never before seen any movement so clearly communicate a collective identity and ideals that spoke directly and personally to me. Everyone who would choose to be involved now had a set of guiding principles. They had values to steer them and move them forward. This is what had been lacking in Washington and - closer to home - in our state capital of Frankfort. The people in positions of power in our government had lost touch with their core beliefs and replaced those principles with politics.

These simple nine principles and twelve values provided a new direction and a common set of ideas. They provided a filter through which the hundreds of thousands of newly-invigorated citizens could view their world and all its assorted complexities. They were the threads that began to knit a budding movement together. When put into practice, these principles and values would become a non-political movement made up of ordinary people like you and me. Concerned citizens from all walks of life could come together around these beliefs. Together they could foster an idea based on values, a movement founded on principles, and a feeling of unity and pride. The same unity and pride that we had all felt as Americans coming together on September 12, 2001 - the day after the shocking attacks on our nation - was a goal worth striving for every day of every year.

Following the presentation of the principles and values, Glenn Beck made a simple request that garnered an overwhelming response. He asked anyone who could agree with at least seven of the nine principles to send him their picture. He was soon flooded with the testimonies of those who agreed along with their photos which would come together to form a larger mosaic image. After all, a single picture is just a picture, but thousands or now over a million placed together can make a powerful statement.

The nine principles and twelve values were immediately relatable to Lydia and I, and we were in agreement with them all. We did exactly what Glenn had invited us to do next. I took a picture of the two of us and sent it off to New York. I am not sure if it was a part of Glenn's master plan all along, but that simple act did something at a subconscious level that I had not anticipated. Sending our picture personalized everything that was going on, and it gave faces to it: our faces.

It is easy for most people to intellectually agree with a movement or to emotionally support a cause. The harder part is finding that extra motivation within yourself to finally turn your intellectual or emotional participation into action. Purchasing bags of pork rinds and delivering them to the local radio station had been a baby step to get us moving. Submitting our picture to be included in giant collage of 9/12 supporters provided us with an initial personal connection, but the next action that we were considering would represent a much longer stride in our journey.

Glenn Beck was encouraging viewers to gather in groups to watch an upcoming special broadcast of his television show on March 13th. To facilitate the forming of these groups, he was encouraging people to host viewing parties in their local communities. For the entire week after the announcement of the broadcast, Lydia and I discussed whether or not we should host one of these events in our area. In the end, we decided we had to continue to follow our instincts, and those instincts were telling us that we needed to jump in and do this.

We were in agreement that we would host a group, but our immediate obstacle was figuring out exactly what that role entailed for us. Details about the special episode itself were sketchy, and what exactly one does at a viewing party was still unknown. Even two years later, that one is still somewhat unknown, I suppose. It was mainly the continuing feeling of isolation that drove both of us to make the leap and serve as hosts. I can honestly say I was not going into the planning of this event looking to be the leader of anything, but I now realize I was actually looking for - and hoping to find - a support group.

More important than the fact that I was not looking to become any sort of political figurehead was the fact that I was completely unqualified to become one in the first place. I was not involved in local politics in Kentucky at all. I did not have the social network of an activist. My wife and I were homebodies who had kept to ourselves and had been perfectly happy to enjoy our time on the sofa together. We had only lived in Kentucky for a couple of years, and we did not even have much in the way of a base of friends locally.

Essentially, we did not know if anyone would even show up if we had a viewing party, but we knew it was up to us to try. It was up to us to stop sitting on that sofa, throwing shoes at the television in frustration, and get up and do something. We decided to trust - not the government or the media - but the people of our community. We sent out a blanket invitation to anyone that wanted to join us to watch Glenn Beck's show on March 13th.

Looking back, our first step either illustrated our complete faith in humanity or our momentary lack of common sense. We sent out an e-mail inviting total strangers into our home to watch television with us. If we had thought that concept through a little bit more at the time, we might never have done anything. In truth, though, we were finally to the point that we wanted to do *something*. Even if that something meant we could possibly be asking an axe murder or some guy with a goat over to our home.

Our initial thinking was that there could possibly be a few other local couples interested in the show, and we would host the viewing party at our house. We put out our contact information on a new web forum that Glenn's show had recommended using. As we posted our information, I noticed the forum already had thousands upon thousands of members, and the discussions about viewing parties in other areas spoke of large venues and estimates of hundreds of people attending. What were we in for?

A few days after we first posted that we wanted to host a viewing party in Kentucky, e-mails started rolling in quickly. Our "few couples" estimate was rapidly turning into fifty or more people. My anxious question to Lydia soon became: "I know we said we would do this…but how?"

My wife is never a quitter, and she would not let this be an obstacle for us. She started brainstorming what we could possibly do to cram fifty or more people into our relatively small ranch-style home. "Maybe if we take the table out and move this and put people there, we could?" She went as far as calculating how many people we could get in front of our four televisions spread throughout the house, including the television in our bedroom!

This was one of the few times in our marriage where I was actually the voice of reason. We realized that the public response had outgrown our home's capability as a venue. Our eleven-inch television in a guest bedroom was not going to cut it.

Finding a new venue, though, proved to be a real challenge. When we called places and attempted to explain exactly what we were looking for, we discovered it could be a little difficult to explain. Imagine you are the owner of a venue and you get this call:

"Hello! I am calling on behalf of a group of strangers that have never met in person, but have made arrangements on the internet to gather together for the first time on March 13th. We are looking for a place where we can watch a TV news show that is not about the news at all really. We are not an official organized group, actually. We have never done anything like this before. Oh, and even though we don't really know each other yet, there may be anywhere from twenty to one hundred of us that show up. It is not exactly anything political in nature, and we are far from being radicals. But…oh yeah…when people come in and try to find our meeting room, they will use the phrase "unite or die" to identify they are with us, and you can send them our way, okay? Don't worry, though, most of them will spot the drawing of a rattlesnake that we will leave near the door to guide their way and not need to stop for directions at all."

After a long and interesting series of phone calls that closely resembled the exchange described above – and terrified business owners all over town - we eventually found a family-friendly pizza "fun center" that had a room that could seat up to eighty potential attendees of our viewing party. Lucky for us, the owner of this pizza place was a Glenn Beck viewer and our search that appeared hopeless suddenly had a happy ending. He was aware of the special broadcast that was airing and graciously gave us the room for free…and even allowed us to use our rattlesnake sign to point people toward it!

Inception

(noun) the beginning, as of a project or undertaking.

MARCH 2009

As March arrived, we had our location and a growing network of people declaring their intentions to attend. Personally, we had a renewed energy and desire to make this viewing party a reality. Where we once were isolated on our couch feeling alone, we now wanted to get the message out to anyone and everyone to bring as many people together as possible to see we were not alone. I knew excitement was building daily at our house as plans continued to come together, but we still struggled with how to get that call to action out locally.

One of the only things we were missing at this point was a local website to really help promote our event and connect to even more people. To solve that problem, a new website was launched: the "Kentucky – We Surround Them" site. This website not only provided all the information about our viewing party time and place, as well as the ability for people to RSVP online, but also featured a message board which served as a new outlet for people that were excited to become a part of this event. They were signing up to become "members" of this new group and sharing their personal passions and motivations for joining. The message board burst with activity of comments and building dissatisfaction with what was happening in the country. People were obviously searching for solutions and channels for their frustration, because within days of the site's launch, individuals just like me somehow found their way to it and made their voices heard. The immediate result was a wave of RSVP's, message board posts, and new members seemingly every hour.

I spent the majority of the next two weeks replying to e-mails and posting responses on our new web forum in amazement. It was no longer just the isolated voices on the radio that were saying what I had been feeling. These were real people I was reaching out to and making connections. Although it was overwhelming to keep up, the more e-mails that came in, the more I wanted to reach out to others. I began to send out invitations to anyone that I thought may have even the slightest interest.

I was not alone in my promotional efforts, as Lydia got into the mix also. As I was sending out e-mails, she was going to local women's political functions and passing out flyers. I can not stress enough how much outside the comfort zone this was for her. She was getting out among people she didn't really know and promoting an event for which she really didn't have many firm details to share. The driving force behind her efforts was the passion she now felt at having an outlet for the months of frustration that had been building within both of us. She was determined to reach as many others as she possibly could and did not want anyone left out of this opportunity to assemble with people that shared not only our concerns for our country but also our belief in its inherent greatness.

While the promotional work we were doing kept us very busy, any free time that I had was filled with growing anticipation as the date drew nearer. Though we continued to receive a strong response to our online event invitations, I still felt trepidation and wondered how many of those individuals would follow through on those mouse clicks and actually show up on March 13th. In the final days, we were left to anxiously await the broadcast knowing we had done all that we possibly could in promoting the event. It was now up to those individuals that had been invited to take their own step of faith and attend.

Despite our best efforts at planning, the morning of March 13th still arrived to find us scrambling to iron out the potential kinks in our plans. With only five hours left until the episode's airing, we still did not know how we were going to stream audio and video into the room we had booked for evening. It was not that we were this unprepared; it was just that everything had developed so quickly in those final weeks, that we had barely had a moment to catch our breath. It was a few short weeks prior that we were planning on a few other couples watching together with us in our home. We were now in a venue that could accommodate eighty people with a laptop, projector, and a load of wires trying to connect into the room's sound system. After a few panicked trips to the local electronics store, we were ready to go with less than an hour to spare.

We had the room set up for the allowed maximum of eighty seats. We had a homemade sign of the famous broken snake with "unite or die" transcribed across the bottom that my eleven-year-old stepson Aaron had made to direct people toward our room. Thanks to a dynamic compatriot named Lisa Williams, we had a replica of the Kentucky state flag that people could sign as a keepsake of the evening. We stationed a registration table near the door where - despite being very pregnant - Lydia joined Lisa to greet people and try to capture e-mail addresses from everyone. We thought we were as ready as we were going to get, and even then we still did not know what to expect. Soon people started arriving…then even more showed up…and then they started piling in!

LISA WILLIAMS

I guarantee that no group can survive without that one person - often behind the scenes - that keeps the wheels greased. Many times, that person is the "mother figure" of the group that seems to keep everything organized. Our "group mom" is Lisa Williams, though over time she has become much more like my little sister that is always there when I need her. When we publicly announced the viewing party, the first e-mail I received was from Lisa. She did not write to ask for details or our plans for the event, but rather to ask what she could possibly do to help us. This practice of putting the needs of others before their own is something we have seen time and time again from Lisa and her husband Lance. Much like me, Lisa was frustrated with the direction of our country and feared for its future. She had been a long-time listener of Glenn Beck's radio program, so when he trumpeted the call to action, she responded. In every event or activity that our group has ever undertaken, Lisa has been the embodiment of our founding values. All the while, her skilled handling of our travel plans, finances, and administrative tasks has been the largely unseen glue that has held our group together. Knowing Lisa the way I do now, it is no surprise in the least that she stepped up and did whatever needed done at our initial viewing party event.

Inevitably, things didn't run as smoothly as we may have hoped. By the beginning of the program, we had a line down the hallway waiting to enter the room. Our anxiety about whether or not anyone would actually show up was instantaneously replaced by anxiety over how we were going to handle the much-larger-than-anticipated crowd we now had on our hands. Lydia and Lisa wisely abandoned trying to get people registered and just ushered them in as fast as they could. Our room with eighty seats now had over one hundred people in it!

At the last second, we were able to claim another room of the pizza place with forty more seats, and quickly filled it as well. Demonstrating the gracious spirit embodied by so many attending that day, all across room, people gave up their seats and were willing to stand for the entire broadcast to allow others to have a comfortable seat. Once everyone was settled at the broadcast was airing, some unavoidable technical difficulties flared up. The streaming web video froze up momentarily a couple of times, which invariably caused me to experience sheer panic, but did not seem to bother anyone else much.

Ultimately, we found out that the inconveniences did not matter at all. Thankfully for us, the people that came that day really did not have any expectations other than "getting together." We also discovered that people jumped in without even having to be asked and helped out anywhere they could, whether it was moving tables and chairs or mingling and gathering e-mail addresses. It turned out that the previously unknown bond that brought us all to that viewing party became a true bond that we shared while we were there. By the end of the one-hour broadcast, most people there now felt like family.

That initial feeling was both exciting and overwhelming. As I have said before, all I was really looking for this gathering to provide was a support group. It was an amazing emotion to go from just one month prior thinking we were all alone to now having literally seen a line of people forming to join you. The event could have ended before the broadcast even started and we would have been satisfied with what we accomplished. Even more rewarding than the sense of reaching a goal we had set was the discovery of newfound friends and a newly-extended "family."

For the people that came together in that pizza place, the atmosphere is something that will always be remembered. From the opening moments of the show, where Glenn Beck delivered a powerful and teary-eyed monologue that has become the broadcast's most lasting image, the air of our room was thick with emotion. As the episode progressed, there were cheers of enthusiasm, outbursts of laughter, moments of silence, and times of excitement. To anyone looking in from the outside, this was over 140 people that spontaneously came together to watch a television show at 5pm on a Friday night. But for us, it was much more. We were not alone.

While we watched together in Lexington, Kentucky, these viewing parties were being duplicated all around the nation. There were cities where thousands assembled together and areas where crowds spilled over to parking lots because they could not fit into their planned venue. There were also countless families who carried out our initial plan and invited other couples into their homes to watch together.

During the course of the broadcast, a new national 9/12 Project web address was announced and flashed upon the screen. In the minutes that followed, an estimated fifty thousand visits to the site were attempted *per second!* The incredible surge in internet traffic shut down an entire wing of servers hosting the site for over two days. Even with the unstable servers, over six hundred thousand unique visitors checked out the website in its first weekend online. In less than one week, over one million people, myself included, had chosen to click a button on the site which indicated their desire to become a member of The 9/12 Project and their agreement with its bedrock principles and values.

We had all answered the call from Glenn Beck, and…no, we were not alone. We all had that feeling in our gut that we needed to do something to create opposition to what was happening in our country. Our frustration and anger was slowly being transformed into determination and excitement.

We had a choice to be the people of September 10, 2001 and bury our heads in the sand or we could be the people of September 12, 2001 and be united again. This was not about Republicans or Democrats. This was not about politics at all. We actually believed in something and we had long-thought our representatives did as well. We had been let down by government, but now stopped wondering how this happened and decided to come together and focus on the things that mattered.

Our hope one month before was just to try and bring people together. Roughly two-thirds of the way through the viewing party, though, it dawned on me that the hundred-plus people in attendance may have had a different idea. Those people might actually look to *me* to say something when the broadcast ended. Human nature could lead people to seek further validation for showing up, encouragement to keep going, and maybe even guidance on what they could do next.

Guess what…I didn't even have those answers myself! I furiously jotted down a few bullet points that I had personally gleaned from the show and patiently waited for the big "pay-off moment" that was sure to come at the end of the show in Glenn's parting thoughts. I was certain that Glenn and his staff had assembled an elaborate diagram or website or chart with easy-to-follow directions that we could all digest and discuss. We would all have a clear roadmap for the journey to restore our republic that we were all so anxious to begin. What was I worried about? There were sure to be so many talking points and instructions for us that discussions would just erupt all over the room. Glenn had my back here. I was sure of it.

At last, the big reveal moment arrived. What were his final words to the assembled masses looking for the next step in this new journey? "We are exactly six months away from 9/12…I would like to ask you to join me on Saturday, 9/12, and I will share what I have been working on to put the principles and values to work in my life… we will meet back here in six months, thank you and good night." Wait! What?! Come on, Glenn, I need more than that! Drop some breadcrumbs for me here, please. What do we do *next*?

Looking back now, I truly believe that if Glenn Beck had gone ahead and spelled out a detailed plan that we needed to follow, both that plan and our project would have failed. This event was never about receiving any "marching orders." It was about personal responsibility. Glenn himself, I believe, never wanted to be our "leader," just the catalyst to inspire us. If I would have only paid closer attention through the years, he has repeatedly said to never believe or do anything because he says so, but to always think and verify everything with your own research.

This was totally to be about grassroots efforts with no centralized master plan. No leader to tell anyone what they were required to do. No formalized structure to obstruct the organic growth from the ground up. There were some important things that we did now have, though. We had a common idea based on principles and values. We had empowerment to act on our own, and we had a support group and network of like-minded patriots to stand by our side.

But all that didn't let me off the hook as the show ended. I still had to say something to the assembled crowd. While I may not have gotten the crystal clear direction from Glenn Beck that I had hoped for, I did have the notes I had taken during his entire broadcast to lean on now. When I looked down at the paper in front of me, these were the thoughts I had captured in writing as I watched:

> *"To succeed, we need to create a foundation. There are a lot of frustrated people wanting to do something, but we can not put the cart before the horse. What was the only difference between the French Revolution and the American Revolution? The American Revolution was based on ideals, while the French was based on anger at bureaucracy and class envy. I fear if we had our revolution, we may be closer to the second. We need to take a step back and build our foundation. We need to get back to the basics. We need to build on the principles and values this country was founded on. We need to understand who we are to better understand what we want. And from this, we will have the ideas to go forward. Like Reagan said, every great change begins at the dinner table. Tonight, this is our dinner table, and look around you, this is your family. Tonight, change begins."*

Standing in front of everyone, my first profound words were "well, I guess we will be getting back together six months from now…and judging from this crowd, and what has happened in a few short weeks… we will need to rent Rupp Arena and we will fill it!" I managed to add a few more comments, and we had a great discussion among the entire group. The best thing we did after our planned event ended was encouraging everyone to stick around and divide into smaller groups to meet other people there from their individual hometowns or communities. Though the official broadcast had finished airing at 6pm, there was still a sizable portion of the group enjoying each other's company and having lively conversations when the pizza place began closing up for the night hours later. Without exactly realizing it, we were empowering people to build interpersonal connections, and these relationships and networks would then continue to develop on their own.

The other great thing we did that day was capture a group photo after the event. It was a huge challenge in itself trying to get 140 people positioned and organized for a picture with other pizza patrons walking by. Not to mention the fact that everyone had already been there for more than an hour in an overcrowded room. We finally got everyone situated and the resulting image is still my favorite picture we have taken to date. It perfectly captured our initial group of fired-up patriots and the start of a fired-up movement.

At the same time that we were setting The 9/12 Project in motion, there was another type of movement brewing locally. When Rick Santelli had called for a "Chicago Tea Party," some people took him seriously. Around the country, community groups were following through on Rick's promise and having tea party-themed rallies to call for greater fiscal responsibility from the federal government. Much like gathering for our viewing party had helped our group begin to form bonds and shift from feelings of anger to feelings of determination; these tea parties were serving a similar purpose for the people attending. In central Kentucky, Leland Conway announced on his radio program that he was making plans for a tea party event in Lexington. Much to my surprise, I received a phone call to help out and be part of a planning meeting for the event.

Why not, right? I clearly had tons of experience in planning large political rallies. Okay, maybe not. As it turned out, it was not my personal charisma they were after. Thanks to the turnout for our viewing party, Leland and the other organizers had already begun to see our Kentucky 9/12 Project as a group that could mobilize people. I didn't have the heart to tell them that I had very little, if anything, to do with it. The crowd just showed up! Nevertheless, Leland had already received phone calls to his radio show from some of the people who had attended our event. Their stories of the friendly and inspiring atmosphere and overflow crowd were exactly what the local tea party organizers were hoping to replicate.

Within a few days, I gathered with five other individuals around a large table over a lunch hour to plan the first central Kentucky tea party. The first discussions centered on lining up the items we would need for the rally and deciding on the speakers. Given my lack of prior participation in these sorts of social actions, I knew virtually nothing about the requirements for a public rally and little more about the speakers that were being suggested at the meeting.

The names included people that were active in Kentucky's liberty preservation effort long before it even became a recognized movement. These were individuals who had made runs for governor, had run conservative "think tanks," or were state directors for national organizations. At the same time, these were not the traditional party insiders. They were liberty-minded conservatives that were many times dismissed by the establishment. This was all part of a whole new culture that I was being exposed to for the first time, but I quickly discovered that the thoughts and beliefs of its practitioners were closely aligned to my own.

As the meeting wrapped up, the discussion turned to getting people to attend the rally and how many should be expected. Leland half-jokingly posed a challenge for me to have at least one hundred of the people from our viewing party now make a return appearance at this tea party event. Whether it was just the excitement of the meeting or my attempt at justifying my inclusion in it, I accepted his challenge and made the statement that the Kentucky 9/12 Project would have at least one hundred people at the tea party.

How naive I was! Why would I ever imagine I could speak for dozens of individual voices? Then again, why would I ever underestimate our new band of 9/12ers? Regardless of the inherent wisdom of my hasty pledge, we now had our next event to promote to our recently developed distribution list. I sent out e-mails, posted details on the internet, and asked everyone to bring signs that read "we are not alone."

The first tea party rally in Kentucky kicked off with my stepson Aaron leading the crowd in the pledge of allegiance in full colonial garb including a tri-cornered hat. There was a sea of signs bouncing in the air above the excited crowd. Much to my personal delight, some of them actually read "we are not alone." The folks that turned out were energized and ready to be pumped up by the speakers. I happened to be one of those speakers and, even though addressing a crowd of this size was completely foreign to me, I enthusiastically gave it all I had. My brief five-minute speech began "I never imagined that I would ever in my life be speaking in front of an angry mob…." I don't recall exactly what I followed that up with, but the crowd applauded and I made it off the stage without embarrassing myself in any way, which was my personal goal for the day.

This rally also served as my first introduction to Jeff Smith, fondly known as "Mario" by many of his friends. The event was in full swing and every speaker was penciled in to address the crowd for about eight minutes. Listening to each person as they took the stage served as my personal crash course in identifying those leading players in the Kentucky liberty movement that I would continue to encounter going forward.

During one of the speaker's remarks, a man came up to Leland and me and asked if he could read a poem to the crowd. This guy looked like he had just ridden in on a Harley-Davidson with his large handlebar mustache, leather jacket, and colorful bandana. Thankfully, this was Leland's event, so I did not have to come up with a polite way to keep this fellow off the stage. Despite my own second (and even third) thoughts about the wisdom of giving him a live microphone, Leland introduced Jeff "Mario" Smith and his poem to the crowd. The following moments were both unexpected and amazing. This rough and tough guy offered an incredibly touching poem brimming with patriotism and honor for our soldiers. He immediately gained my respect, and in the near future he would become both a fellow 9/12er and a personal friend.

JEFF SMITH

Jeff "Mario" Smith was a veteran and patriot with a son serving in Iraq. He was also one those people that had been well aware of the political realities before a lot of us were waking up. Long before there was a 9/12 Project, he had been writing letters, speaking about what was wrong, and standing up for liberty. Unfortunately, like many others that felt as if they had been battling on their own for far too long, he began to tune out. His dogged determination was replaced with frustration. The day of the first Kentucky tea party was one of many turning points that helped him renew his energy. Although he was not officially in the program, there was no doubt he was there. He had a flair for events like this and for something he came to call "guerilla politics." This meant fighting back with sometimes unconventional methods and occasionally in arenas that were occupied by the opposition. You would find him not only speaking passionately at tea parties and events, but his writings would show up as letters to the editor in more liberal newspapers and postings on internet blogs. "Mario" is one of the most active and vocal supporters that the Kentucky 9/12 Project could have ever hoped to find and his experience in fighting for personal responsibility and individual liberty has been invaluable to the group.

There were a couple of important memories that I took away from my initial tea party experience. The first one was the atmosphere of the event. Even though the people making up the crowd of around 1,500 people were frustrated and irritated about things that were going on in Washington and this was supposed to be a "protest" rally, these folks were smiling and in a good mood. Even though the media was actively painting us as an angry and unreasonable mob, that portrayal could not have been further from reality. This event felt more like a neighborhood family festival than a heated protest. Perhaps that was an indication that none of us fit the "unruly demonstrator" mold exactly, but we wanted to make our combined voices heard in any way that we could. While our motivation was a growing disgust with the state of affairs in our government, everyone remained pleasant and anyone would have been comfortable in that crowd.

The second memory was how important the tea party event was in helping everyone quickly come to accept the Kentucky 9/12 Project as a legitimate liberty group. Our scattered signs and symbols were clearly evident among the crowd on that day. There were many people that showed up not only because they were a part of this new Tea Party movement, but were also proud supporters of the 9/12 Project movement as well. As for my promise to add at least one hundred folks to the crowd for the event, I am not sure, nor is it important, exactly how many 9/12ers showed up that day. All I know, for sure, is the 1,500 people in the crowd was a lot more than the two hundred promotional flyers for our group that I had printed out to distribute!

In many ways, this tea party was not a lot different from the initial event we had just completed weeks earlier. It satisfied a need we all had to gather together and continue to see that we indeed were not alone. It provided a catalyst for people to get energized and motivated to take action. Finally, it helped push those in attendance across the threshold from feelings of anger to feelings of determination.

In some other key ways there were differences from our viewing party, too. The tea party was less about personal responsibility and more about government accountability. Due to the size of the crowd, the atmosphere was not as intimate as an overcrowded banquet room in a pizza parlor. It did not have the foundation of a clearly defined set of common principles and values that our 9/12 theme provided. Fiscal responsibility was the clear message of the day, but in the context it was used, it was an issue and not a value.

Like nearly all the rest of us, Leland Conway and the other event organizers had never done anything like a public rally before, either. Without question, though, the birth of the organized Tea Party movement in Kentucky can be traced back to this rally's success. A newly united network of activists and radio listeners emerged from the day, and that network would yield huge benefits in the future advancement of the overall liberty movement in our state.

∽

APRIL 2009

As April arrived, we were at a stage where we had an idea based on principles and values, a push for personal responsibility, and a developing support group and network of like-minded patriots. Back at our initial viewing party's conclusion, we had taken time to separate into small groups with others from our individual communities. I mentioned before that things began developing on their own as a result of the community breakouts. We had hoped people would have a desire to meet again, and that is exactly what happened.

In the weeks that followed the viewing party, local meetings were being planned and other people were stepping up and taking on leadership roles in their individual towns. The first of these new local meetings took place in Danville, Kentucky on April 6th and was led by a man named Jim Fishback. In these early local meetings, our goal was simply to promote our founding principles and values as a common set of beliefs that could unite people in our communities, and the local leaders did the best they could to accomplish that objective. Just like with the first viewing party event, though, the new people that were waking up and coming out for the first time didn't have any pre-set expectations beyond hoping to meet other concerned folks in their area.

We believe this was what our Founding Fathers intended, and this was what The 9/12 Project was going to be all about. Our country wasn't founded by a tea party or a political action committee, but rather by a preservation committee of sorts. It was people coming together locally and educating each other. More and more people were learning about our Kentucky 9/12 Project, and more importantly finding a family unit and forming their own preservation committees.

The town of Danville is over one hour's drive from the pizza place that hosted our first viewing party, so at this local meeting we had quite a few new faces. For some of these folks, it was their introduction to the group even though they may have watched the March 13th broadcast from their homes. For others, it was a welcomed reunion with individuals they had already bonded with the prior month.

Just days after this Danville event launched our local group concept, Jeff and Lisa Abler started meetings in our hometown of Georgetown, Kentucky. Lydia and I made certain to arrive early and were excited to see people start coming in and once again filling another room. Given how close our town is to Lexington, many of the folks showing up were familiar faces we now recognized as new friends we had made at the viewing party and had been looking forward to seeing again.

More local meetings followed, and within the first two weeks of April - notably less than one month from the initial start of our group - we had four local meetings in assorted towns around the state. There were various people rising up and becoming champions in their own communities. After attending the inaugural meeting in each community, we observed that all of them were relatively similar, and in some degree, much like the March 13th meeting, as well. New faces continued to show up in the hope of confirming that they were not alone and going away relieved with that knowledge. These meetings gave people an outlet and - like me - they were no longer sitting at home throwing shoes at televisions. They were now doing something and helping to create an opposition movement to expansive government. Their anger was slowly and surely being converted into determination and excitement. Every local meeting promoted personal responsibility and discovering truths for one's self. The goal of each meeting was always to educate the members and always to remain true to our founding principles and values.

Each of the local groups was empowered to reach out to their communities and advance our movement in their individual areas, but we were searching for an opening to promote our statewide reach to a larger audience. That opportunity came in mid-April at an event called "The Liberty Fair" sponsored by a conservative think tank in Kentucky named The Bluegrass Institute. Their concept was a fabulous idea, and the event was well-executed. The drive behind the event was to reach the large number of people just waking up to the political realities and getting off their sofas for the first time with a fun family event that they could come out and explore. The goal was to have a few inspiring speakers and to allow multiple local liberty groups to set up booths and activities to let people know the sorts of groups that were out there and find one that fit them.

This was perfect timing for the people choosing to get politically active and also excellent timing for a recently developing movement like our 9/12 Project. The problem we faced was that we had no real group structure and zero money for the booth space. Luckily, KY9/12 was not just Lydia and I, and there were other people that believed in our group even though we were an unknown commodity to most at this point. Those people saw the importance of this event for us, and the generosity of our members made its first appearance. Amazingly, without us asking anyone, someone purchased a booth space on our behalf. They called me up about two weeks before the event and told me we had a space to use. Now what would we do with it?

Two infinitely valuable lessons came out of this event. First, I discovered something that should have been obvious to me given the fact that Lydia kept explaining it to me: I had to trust the people in the group. We now had two weeks and no ideas or promotional items for a booth. I sent an e-mail out to the group asking for volunteers, resources, tables, ideas, anything. HELP!

Having complete faith that our members would come to the rescue should have had me prepared, but their swift response overwhelmed my expectations. First, one member suggested a theme of "Liberty and Tyranny." Next, we had someone volunteer with a laptop and digital camera to take pictures if we wanted. We even had an amazing member that bought an instant digital printer to be able to print the photos on the spot. We found a table and other necessities and everything was coming together.

Thankfully, there were also members with much more creativity than myself. Setting up the booth, on the side entitled "Liberty" we had a backdrop of a collage of photos. When people attending the fair agreed with at least seven of our nine foundational principles, they could get their picture taken and added to our "We Surround Them" collage to illustrate that they were not alone. Much like sending a picture of Lydia and I to Glenn Beck had done for us, this collage helped people personalize our movement and allowed them to feel part of our group.

On the other side of the booth entitled "Tyranny," a very creative member of our group named Susan Bennett made a set of wooden stocks with signs in front bearing sayings like "don't tax me, bro" or "principled voter." We sold the opportunity to get a photo taken in the stocks to keep as a souvenir. On our table in front, we had pocket Constitutions, hats, and some shirts to give away. We also had a helium tank - which we referred to ironically as the "Inflation Station" - to fill balloons to pass out to kids, as well as printed brochures and other materials. All of these items had been donated to our group, and all within two weeks' time. You could have even fooled me that we knew what we were doing and looked legitimate.

SUSAN BENNETT

If you spend more than a couple of minutes talking with Susan Bennett, you are guaranteed to hear some quirky saying that will make you smile. She is a creative and artistic personality that you just can't help but love. Susan was politically active from a very young age but faced a huge reality check when she campaigned vigorously for a certain politician while she was in college. After the election had ended and she had relished the joy of a mission accomplished, the mask came off and her chosen candidate soon revealed himself to be just like all the other career politicians. She wrote a seven-page single-spaced letter to his office that went unanswered and then drifted into apathy with the rest of us. Hearing about our budding movement sparked a new hope inside her. A hope of finding like-minded people that opposed "politics as usual" like she did. My first introduction to Susan happened when she came to the Liberty Fair event dressed as a character in a fluffy blue dress that she called "Alice in Blunderland." More often than not, Susan was the 9/12er that made our events fun, because she had that spirit that others wanted to be around. Unfortunately for us, her work eventually stole her away to Michigan, but her contributions live on as she now serves as an advisory member for the national 9/12 Project.

That brings me to the second valuable lesson that came out of this event. I came to realize that - more than any event, item, or slogan - it was the relationships that were being formed that would prove to be priceless for our Kentucky 9/12 Project. More important than the hundreds of people that came by our booth - and more crucial than the dozens of new members we added to our roles that day - were the volunteers that stepped up on this and other early days in our group's development. Many of these same people are still active in our efforts today.

These were the people that helped develop the core of KY9/12, and these were the people that had the heart and spirit to do the heavy lifting when needed. Something else was happening as well, though. These people were becoming close personal friends and special bonds were being formed. This was not just random people working together. These were people that not only shared an opposition to what was going on in our government, but also shared principles and values and a desire to restore our republic. All these shared beliefs and objectives became the fertile soil of budding lifelong friendships.

JIM & NIKI DRAKE

As the curtain is pulled back and you begin to see politics and politicians for who they are, cynicism begins to set in. The 2008 election season was the final straw for Jim and Niki Drake. By that point, they had feelings of suspicion and anger with everything going on in our government. They also shared our common nagging desire to try to right the ship of our republic and bring principles back. They came to the first viewing party at the pizza place with cautious hope. Looking back now, they tell me that after we met at the initial viewing party, they sensed that I was someone who was "in it" for the right reason and they decided to become more involved out of respect for that feeling. What they may not have realized, though, is that it was the many discussions they had with Lydia and I that served to give me clear perspectives on issues and encouraged me to keep going. Both Jim and Niki have been there from the beginning and are key reasons why I am still here, as well. They have become much more than fellow members, as they are now true friends and the first people I lean on when internal issues arise. They both have different personalities with Jim being the logic-driven intellectual and Niki being the fiery "tell-you-like-it-is" spirit. Together, they are the perfect sounding board, and I know we all share the same 9/12 spirit and values deep in our hearts.

We did make our share of mistakes in these early months, but there was a key to everything we were doing. Our key was making the best of every situation and finding a way to make it work. All the while, we were building relationships and building a movement.

Of course, we did have the more radical elements among us that wanted us to become something we were not. We also had the people that jumped on what they perceived as a bandwagon in an attempt to use our group for themselves in an act of self-promotion. These misguided individuals were far outnumbered by hundreds of principled people and a core group that I now called friends. We now had more than a foundation…and even though it had happened virtually overnight…we had a movement. We had the Kentucky 9/12 Project.

Identity

(noun) the individual characteristics by which a person or
thing is recognized.

MAY 2009

While things rapidly came together here in Kentucky, similar events were occurring across the nation with other groups as well. Together, we were "setting brush fires in people's minds" and a new more-determined majority was waking from their previous apathy and isolation. Though we all shared a common set of guiding principles and proudly referred to ourselves collectively as "9/12ers," we were all going in our respective directions following the initial viewing on March 13th. There were no textbooks on what we were to do next and no "top down" structure at a national level steering us as one large ship. Instead, we were more like dozens of tiny rowboats paddling around the ocean without a compass. Thankfully, our Kentucky rowboat was quickly filling up with new "rowers" anxious to grab an oar and get to work!

Only a couple of months after having a desire to get a few people together to watch a Glenn Beck episode for mostly self-serving reasons, we now had a recognized group complete with a website and members that wanted to do something. At this point, I couldn't have told you how we got to where we were much less what we were going to do next. Thus we did what every new fledgling group - not quite sure of who or what it is - probably does in that position: we did anything and everything, but mostly went around in circles.

Our people clearly had legitimate passion and sincere desire for change now. In the absence of any recognized leader or direction at this point, we saw the rise of good-intentioned people recommending what we needed to do next. The suggestions began to roll in to do this event or tackle that issue or jump on board with whatever other groups happened to be doing at the moment. This gave us a new shotgun approach to our actions. We were really trying to find our identity, but at the same time, we were "scratching the itch" of our members to fulfill their passions and be busy doing something *now*.

My goal at this point was still not necessarily to be a leader of a movement but to just bring this group of people to Washington, D.C. on September 12th and back home safely. Being naïve again, I had no idea what was beyond that or the ideas that were being planted. My thoughts were focused on the present, and the conclusion at that time was that if things were to be fixed, we all had to become activists. What I didn't realize was that I was shooting for short-term gains and only reacting to the next issue or bad piece of legislation that came out of Washington. Our thoughts revolved around what we would do the following week or what event we would plan next. In hindsight, even though I was focused on providing a better future for my children, I never stopped to consider what tools I was giving them or what foundation I was providing them, but instead chased the issue of the day. Ultimately, the struggles and lack of focus we did endure in the summer and fall of 2009 would help to make us a stronger group with a clearer identity…. if we had the fight and conviction to survive it.

So fight we did! We made phone calls, wrote letters, read books, held rallies, and went door to door with our message. We also got creative with picnics, charity professional wrestling, and posting lost dog posters to call out our "blue dog" congressman during the town hall season.

Clearly, not everything we were doing during this period of time had a logical fit. While many of our activities produced positive results, I am not certain when looking back now how some of those activities were really the best uses of our energy and influence. There are some excellent groups in Kentucky that do wonderful work in specific areas, and for us to duplicate efforts and rally support or organize rallies for every isolated issue that a few members felt passionate about would eventually run our group ragged. Even if someone proposed we follow through on Benjamin Franklin's desire to see the turkey rather than the eagle as our national symbol, "Gobble-Up Signatures Saturday" spent getting petitions signed while wearing feathered costumes would not necessarily be the best use of our collective time. With that said, I confess that I would likely have been the first one to don a bird suit and join them.

Thankfully, we were able to find plenty of more reasonable activities in which to invest our combined time and energy. In an effort to improve our effectiveness as a group, we decided to put a special emphasis on personal responsibility and self-education. This would turn out to be some of the best seeds we could have planted early on that would grow to radically change our movement over time. The commitment to learning more every day gave us all the personal foundation that would be called upon in the coming months. Our dedicated membership in Kentucky began a period of voracious reading and self-discovery. While our organized efforts at promoting certain authors and books to our members may have helped motivate a few of them to start reading, a larger majority had already begun this process on their own. That thirst for knowledge was a common theme in our discussions, as many of us came to realize how many things about our own history and our founders we had never learned in school or elsewhere in life.

Members picked up a wide range of books like "Rules for Radicals," "Atlas Shrugged," "The Real George Washington," and countless others. We absorbed information about our nation's heritage, studied what the progressive movement was doing, and changed the way in which we thought. Having seen the power of personal responsibility in action, I firmly believe that it is a commitment to self-education that does more to create long-lasting and motivated individuals in our social movement than anything that is ever presented in a group setting.

In order to stoke the enthusiasm for education, we decided to host a "Making of America" seminar based on the book "The 5000 Year Leap." Glenn Beck had mentioned previously that this was the book that woke him up, and it was highlighted on the March 13th broadcast as well. This made the seminar both a great fit and easy sell for our membership.

The "Making of America" seminars are presented by the National Center for Constitutional Studies (NCCS). I had received information on their organization from a much larger 9/12 group in Cincinnati, Ohio who were slightly ahead of our Kentucky group in their own growth and development. When we called the NCCS to schedule our seminar, we learned that we would need to commit to having fifty paid attendees to book a conference date. The date we had announced was only two weeks away and there were only seventeen people registered. We decided to go ahead and officially book the conference by sending in the five hundred dollars required and trust that enough of our members would make the decision to attend to keep us from losing money.

After all, it seemed like a perfect fit for us, remember? Thankfully, we were not disappointed. The course material emphasized and magnified the very principles and values on which The 9/12 Project had been founded. There was indeed good reason for us to have recommended "The 5000 Year Leap" for our entire group's personal reading lists. For those same reasons, we still do these seminars regularly in our local communities today.

Many of us were just waking up to the true state of affairs in American government, and we were hopelessly unarmed with facts and ignorant to our own history. This training gave us the understanding of where we came from and also where we went wrong. It helped everyone to identify where the fork in the road had been and which path should have been chosen. It helped give us a stronger grasp on history and the drive to communicate it to others. More importantly, it provided us with the firm foundation of knowledge of our timeless founding principles.

This staggering influx of information struck different chords with the various people in attendance. Some found they were inspired after hearing the true story of how America was made and the struggles of the founders to discover the principles of freedom. Many left wanting to share these amazing stories with their friends and neighbors so everyone would have a similar deep appreciation for our nation. Still others, including my wife Lydia, found they were actually somewhat discouraged after absorbing the conference material. Understanding now what the founders truly created for this country and seeing the principles that once meant something, they now had a better appreciation of how far our nation had fallen. They were frustrated and disheartened by not knowing how we could ever get back there again.

The seminar was worth every penny we put into it, but for us, it had been another leap of faith. We had no funds and no guarantees that anybody would actually show up. Sure, at this point we had established a pretty good track record of people coming out for our events. The big difference here was the fact that we were charging for admission to one of our events for the first time…and we were going to be out over one thousand dollars if no one came. Remember, we had zero dollars, so having people attend was imperative to keep me in the good graces of my wife, as well as the core members of our group.

We decided to trust in our tried-and-true formula for success. We set up the location, we set up an event website, and we promoted the event. We sent invitations to anyone and everyone then prayed and hoped someone would show up. We needed forty-five paid attendees to cover our out-of-pocket expenses. When the doors were closed and the seminar began, we had sixty amazing people that showed up on a Saturday to spend their entire day going "back to school" on their nation's founding. Those sixty people kept the Kentucky 9/12 Project out of the red ink, and kept me out of the doghouse at home.

ᘒ

SUMMER 2009

Not everything we threw our energy behind was quite the ideal fit for our group that the "Making of America" seminar proved to be. Don't get me wrong, we had several other great events that exceeded our expectations. There were, of course, other times we found ourselves disappointed and forced to realize something we had planned may not have made complete sense for our group. Even those less successful ventures were entertaining and likely contributed to our group's growth in some fashion, but they helped fill our summer with a sense of chaos.

In the summer of 2009, there was an outdoor liberty rally in Kentucky almost every weekend. While many of our members were actively attending these events on their own, there was a growing desire for our group to put our own spin on things. We soon concluded we would actually plan and host our own tea party rally.

We wanted something to set our event apart from the others happening around the area, so we used the anniversary of Kentucky gaining statehood to gather people in Georgetown. The turnout was encouraging, and we even encountered our very first protestor attending one of our functions. This particular woman was well-known in the community thanks to her colorful personality, which she often displayed while making phone calls to local talk radio programs. Her announced attendance at our rally actually helped us in securing valuable publicity that we would have not received otherwise. Knowing she would attend - instead of excluding her or squaring off with her - we set up a recliner reserved especially for her right in front and did our best to make her feel welcome.

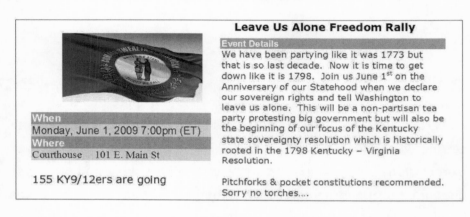

Leave Us Alone Freedom Rally

Event Details

We have been partying like it was 1773 but that is so last decade. Now it is time to get down like it is 1798. Join us June 1st on the Anniversary of our Statehood when we declare our sovereign rights and tell Washington to leave us alone. This will be a non-partisan tea party protesting big government but will also be the beginning of our focus of the Kentucky state sovereignty resolution which is historically rooted in the 1798 Kentucky – Virginia Resolution.

When
Monday, June 1, 2009 7:00pm (ET)
Where
Courthouse   101 E. Main St

155 KY9/12ers are going

Pitchforks & pocket constitutions recommended. Sorry no torches....

On the heels of a well-received rally in Georgetown, we embraced the great outdoors and promoted our first annual family picnic at a local historic winery. This was our calculated attempt to try to recapture the spirit of our initial March 13th gathering by creating our own family-friendly, "semi-non-political" event to bring people back together to continue to see that they were not alone. In the months that had passed since our group's formation, our members had been in a relentless state of vigilance. We had held tea parties, liberty fairs, and freedom rallies. We had met in homes and neighborhoods, made phone calls, and become more active in the political process. Now we just wanted to say thanks and give everyone permission to take a break and catch their breath for the day.

While the brilliant sunshine and gorgeous scenery provided an ideal backdrop for our picnic, the heat provided some challenges for those in attendance. Lydia was eight months pregnant, and she was coming out to a ninety-degree day with little available shade. Doing basically anything in the final month of a pregnancy is an uncomfortable experience, so sitting in the heat for hours was rough. True to her personality, she did not let the elements discourage her and shared my excitement for the day.

The picnic provided an atmosphere of fellowship and encouragement for all those in attendance. As we watched our children run and play together through the vineyard fields, we were reminded exactly who it was that we were all working for in the end. I remember personally pausing to watch my daughter Sarah enjoying the day with a group of other girls around her age. In that moment, I resolved in my heart to continue to promote the principles and values of our group in every possible way to ensure those girls could grow up with all the same freedoms and opportunities that I had long taken for granted.

The atmosphere and spirit of the picnic was uplifting, but there were lighter moments as well. We had an entertaining performance from an eleven-year-old singing prodigy. We also had a chicken biscuit eating contest. Yes, you read that last sentence correctly. The competitive eating portion of the show was venturing well beyond the bounds of our comfort zone, but you have not lived until you get to watch grown men try to devour a plate of dry chicken biscuits under the blistering heat of the sun. A 9/12er named Justen Collins took home the title of chicken biscuit king that afternoon and earned himself the unofficial

designation of "publicity stuntman" for the Kentucky 9/12 Project. He
would be called upon a few more times in the near future.

When we weren't playing around in the hot sun that summer, our
group was sending out action items for our members to contact their
congressman and make their voices heard. We attacked every issue
from cap and trade to auditing the Federal Reserve. We generated
phone calls and e-mails from our group on issues from amnesty for
illegal aliens to the year's biggest issue: health care.

The health care debate really hit home for us, in particular, as we
sat in a hospital room with Sophia, our beautiful newborn baby girl. As
the tensions surrounding the issue were rising to new levels, we were
watching it all unfold on 24-hour news between the 20-minute naps the
baby was taking. Witnessing the founding principles and Constitution
being ignored or even trampled on, we both knew we had to ignore the
limitations of being a new parent and do something. Again, we were not
alone. Everyone was hungry for this fight, and as a group, we needed
to have our voices heard. We planned our next event right there in a
hospital recovery room.

We attacked the health care issue with the same gusto as we
approached everything we did. The concept we chose to employ was
an idea that Lydia suggested. The rallies and town hall meetings that
were being planned elsewhere were great, but it was like attending
church in some ways. You could hear a great message and at times
seem to be on the verge of a good old-fashioned revival. You might
walk away inspired, but in many ways, we were all preaching to the choir.
What was really needed - more than ever - was more missionaries. We
all needed to become our own spokesman for liberty and truth in our
local communities. With this desire in mind, we organized a "Walk to
Free Our Health Care" campaign. We encouraged people to take a

weekend and go visit one hundred homes in their neighborhood, knock on doors, create public awareness about this issue, and ask people to call their representatives.

Information about this initiative quickly traveled from one 9/12 group to another and, much to our surprise, walks were being organized in Ohio, Tennessee, Florida, Texas, Pennsylvania, North Carolina, Arizona, Utah, and Oklahoma, and those are just the states we heard from directly. Coverage of these events was the Kentucky 9/12 Project's first highlighted exposure on the national 9/12 Project website. We were amazed that an idea conceived by Lydia and initiated by KY9/12 was being implemented nationwide to some extent.

As a result of this joint effort across the country, it is estimated that over eighty thousand homes were visited over two weekends. Many of the doors swung open to receptive audiences that shared our concerns about the 2,000-plus page monstrosity of a bill that represented a clear attack on the individual liberties and rights that made our country great. It is a safe assumption that the direct result of the "Walk to Free Our Health Care" was thousands more phone calls made in opposition to government-mandated health care. Closer to home, Lydia and I with our new one-month-old baby Sophia in tow held up our end of the bargain. Despite the sleep-deprivation and fatigue we had to overcome, it was a worthwhile sacrifice for our family to go door-to-door through our neighborhood visiting one hundred homes with our message.

Sadly, during this summer is when we also lost our dog. Yes, our very own "Blue Dog" Democrat Congressman was out of session and back home in Kentucky, but he was no where to be found. "Blue Dogs" is the nickname given to the self-proclaimed fiscally conservative and center-leaning members of the Democrat Party. Our local Congressman was among that group. As other Congressmen across the country were

having town hall meetings with their constituents, ours wouldn't even
return a phone call or be seen in public. Being so worried about him,
we plastered his district with "lost dog" posters on telephone poles,
store windows, and community bulletin boards.

This effort reached a conclusion when two of our members found
our lost dog! They coincidentally encountered our evasive Congressman
while they were posting a lost dog sign on the telephone pole in front
of his home. It was maybe not the best idea, but a bold one. In an
account from one of those members, things did not go as bad as they
could have, and they had a productive impromptu meeting and shared
their concerns directly with the Congressman.

Lost Dog!

**Missing for almost a year now, have you seen
our lost dog?**

Answers to the name: Ben Chandler

Last seen campaigning prior to the last election.

**We accidentally let him out to go to Washington
and have not seen him since.**

**Please if you have seen Ben Chandler
Contact us at KY912.COM**

"Hounding" our Congressman to have the courage to face his constituents was actually not the strangest approach we would take in our summer of chaos. Undoubtedly, one of our more creative events took place inside the famed "squared circle." It is always cause for concern when a radio personality calls you and says, "I have this idea…" For us, that call came from Leland Conway, and his idea consisted of his producer bad-mouthing our 9/12 Project and calling out one of our members, Justen "Big Daddy" Collins aka BDC - The Kentucky Chicken Biscuit Champion. The producer spent weeks talking trash on the air and forcing BDC to defend not only his honor but the honor of KY9/12. Tensions grew as the two of them met up at a local restaurant and exchanged verbal jabs at each other during a 9/12 local meeting. The gauntlet was finally thrown down and there was nothing left to do but for them to meet up in a wrestling ring.

Yes, this was all an elaborate staging for a charity wrestling event with all the proceeds going to the Tennessee / Kentucky Chapter of Operation Homefront, an organization which provides financial assistance to active duty military and wounded warriors, as well as provides care packages to soldiers that are deployed. Thankfully, BDC won the match with his patented "Rocky Top Leg Drop" prompting the producer from the radio show to make a public apology to the Kentucky 9/12 Project and become a member himself. Most importantly, the radio station raised lots of donations for Operation Homefront. Perhaps of equal importance, no one got injured in the process!

JUSTEN COLLINS

Justen "Big Daddy" Collins relocated his family from Tennessee to Kentucky in the fall of 2008 after accepting a job working for the same company as me. As fate would have it, he ended up in the desk next to mine, and we struck up the usual friendly office neighbor relationship. On occasion, our conversations would drift to political or ideological issues, and we discovered we shared many of the same beliefs and values. Justen had recently become a father for the first time, and the new responsibilities of parenthood were causing him to view the current events of the world through a new set of eyes. Having gone from politically active as a student to politically apathetic as a young adult, he now realized that it was part of his role as a good father to show his son what it meant to also be a good citizen. After hearing my stories at work about the early days of KY9/12, Justen began to research our principles and values on his own. He soon realized he had found the perfect outlet for his desire to make a difference for his family's future. He asked me what he could do to help the cause, and that was probably his first mistake! After his first few assignments of eating chicken biscuits in the blazing sun, coming out of his professional wrestling retirement to raise money for charity, and serving as a roadie for our traveling sound system were successfully completed, he settled into a more traditional role for our group. Justen is now the Social Media Coordinator for the Kentucky 9/12 Project and helps coordinate our Facebook, Twitter, and internet outreach. We still work together, too, so he has become a good friend and one of the first people I can turn to when I need a sanity check or listening ear.

I may have painted much of the summer of 2009 in a humorous light, but it was discouraging at times, as well. We were doing a lot of varied events and participation was occasionally meager or underwhelming. There were so many assorted grassroots activities happening across Kentucky in that summer that we allowed our time spent promoting other groups' efforts to sometimes shift the focus away from our own details and planning.

Given my situation at home, it would be ironic to say we were experiencing some "labor pains" in the birth of this new movement. This summer proved challenging for me as well. There were some weeks where I experienced feelings of frustration and dampening resolve. Trying to stay on top of the chaos while keeping my spirits up was proving to be a struggle.

I was going to every event, and it seemed I was seeing the same diehard members all the time. It appeared our group was only as strong as our next event, and it was a select few joining me in coming up with ideas. I was still not an official leader, but the more I put myself in the forefront, the more people continued to look to me to see what was next. I took on answering e-mails, helping with event planning, and promoting the group. I was running myself into the ground and all with a new baby at home. Having my wife Lydia – my biggest supporter – now needing to focus on being a mother to our baby meant I was left to tackle many things on my own. There was a clear need for me to find the right balance of work, family, and a more-defined role in this movement, but during this hectic summer, I was not meeting it.

The crowded calendar created a barrage of event invitations, updates, promotions, and reminders that likely fueled our growing sense of chaos as much as they fueled our group participation. The efforts of the group were really all over the place, and people were beginning to get burnt out by the frantic shifts. At the same time, others expressed frustration that we were not addressing their particular issue or that none of the things we were doing seemed to be working fast enough.

෴

AUGUST 2009

A portion of our events – from holding an "Accountabili-Tea Party" in front of our local newspaper to protest media bias to going Christmas caroling at our state capital to protest the "holiday" tree not being called a Christmas tree to hosting a candlelight vigil the night before a big vote on health care with "miniature torches" – were simply fulfilling a need for action. The constant call of our membership was, "what do we do next?" The true underlying problem was a void in direction.

Rest assured there was no shortage of people that wanted to personally fill that void and many of them for nefarious reasons. I suppose that is not a completely fair statement, as saying "nefarious" would infer an evil intent when most of these people had good intentions or pure passions for certain issues. Their agendas were just not in line with The 9/12 Project or the majority of its members at that point.

At several points in our chaotic summer, self-serving folks were popping up and using our movement to promote themselves or their projects. The leadership void seemed to provide an opportunity to step into an available "spotlight" of sorts, and there were a handful of folks who hoped to capitalize on that platform. Others sought to use our membership to cross-promote their outside group, their blog, or their tea party and never really understood what KY9/12 hoped to be. On the other side of the equation, we did have those that understood our goals and objectives, but disagreed with our methods and made attempts to push us towards more radical activism.

To further complicate matters, all of these different types of individuals had the ability to reach our entire audience of 9/12ers right at their fingertips. Up until this point, we had what was known as an "open" e-mail forum through our website. This simply meant that any person who joined could e-mail the entire membership and any responses would also go to all members. In our formative days, this had been a very beneficial feature that allowed for people to connect, share, and stay informed about our plans. Unfortunately, the open forum now provided a means for the self-servers, radicals, and single-issue supporters to propagate their messages. It had worked fine when we had one hundred members, but having four times as many members now generated dozens upon dozens of e-mails daily.

We arrived at a point where we were losing members directly because of these e-mails, and it was obvious that we had to do something. I guess "obvious" may not be true, because it was this decision that raised the biggest objections. For some, the e-mail forum represented the very spirit that had brought them into our group. This liberty-based attitude of zero censorship and complete freedom fought against any oversight.

These purists of our movement truly believed that progressing to a new format would actually be abandoning the movement. This was the hardest subsection of people we had to deal with because, in many ways, I was in this camp myself. My own instincts leaned toward their decentralized libertarian views, and that was partly the reason we currently had no structure or oversight and were closer to a state of member-led chaos.

With all that said, even I reached a point where it was painful to open my inbox every morning and find forty to fifty e-mails waiting. Roughly half would be from people using or abusing the open forum. An additional few would be messages that should never show up on ours or any site, and the people sending them were likely not even 9/12ers. The remaining e-mails would be people contacting me directly, either to complain about those few or the sheer number of e-mails they were receiving. It was clear action was required, as I spent more of my time apologizing, deleting threads, and telling members to "cool it" than anything else at this point. I was being a babysitter when I needed to step up and become a leader.

The distractions and bickering that were plaguing our group were often originating with a few members on the fringe of our movement. There were inherent dangers involved with letting any of these individuals continue to push their agendas on the membership. The "me" types or self-serving folks would eventually begin to alienate others by making themselves the focal point of events causing people to grow weary of their antics and just stop participating. The "do more" radicals could also scare off members with their demanding personalities and suggestions that sometimes pushed the envelope farther than our group was ready or willing to go. Lastly, the "purists" could endanger the future development of the group with their strict resistance to having any sort of structure or governance to provide direction and leadership for the individuals in our movement.

The self-serving crowd had proven easy to handle. You simply ignored them, gave them time to expose themselves, and others saw their motives. The radicals were often loud, but could be handled without remorse. I could still rest easy at night after banning a member that was on the fringe when it was plain to see they would do damage to the group if left unchecked. With other radicals that continually pushed us to do more, we could resist their efforts by sticking to our principles and they would often leave on their own. Yes, this sometimes led to other splitter groups of activists, but that was not always a bad thing, either. It provided another forum for others that shared those particular desires and motivations. By taking a stand and not supporting their agenda, we were able to use the contrast between our beliefs to better define our separate groups. More importantly, by not supporting or promoting events or initiatives that were outside of our core principles and values, we were insuring we would not dilute the image or reputation of the Kentucky 9/12 Project.

Handling the hard-line purists was where I was struggling most. Addressing the e-mail forum problems required action that I viewed as taking control, and I wanted to resist that aspect myself. Eventually, reality was ushered in after a talk with a Jim Drake – my rational advisor in time of need - which helped remind me that a train wreck on either side of the tracks is equally bad. We could clearly see that by this point our e-mail forum "train" was not even on the tracks anymore!

It became apparent that we had become just "people in a group" and not a "group of people." A social movement can't just be a crowd, because a crowd does not possess any motivational mechanism to sustain membership. There is no organized communication or coordinated activity with a crowd because they lack any sort of centralized network to make them possible. Without those fundamentals, there is no hope for a random crowd of people to ever accomplish any sort of long-term objective.

Groups, on the other hand, have boundaries for a reason and exist for a cause. Our standards in regards to what we would or would not permit were easy for us to define. We already had a set of nine principles and twelve values that we could use to assess any decisions.

Most resounding in those principles was the concept of personal responsibility. It was not the group's responsibility to promote every single issue, nor was it the group's responsibility to maintain an e-mail forum to satisfy the seven percent of the members actively participating on it. We came to the conclusion that if those members wanted an e-mail forum, they needed to create one themselves. If other members wanted to promote a specific issue that they felt we were not devoting enough attention to, they were free to do that on their own, as well.

It had never really been our responsibility to do any of these things. We just did them. In many ways, by trying to be all things to all members, we were taking some of the chances for personal responsibility away from them. It was time to give some of those opportunities back, so we shut down the open e-mail forum for good one evening. We encouraged those members that were interested to start another e-mail group or forum of their own.

Even though the forum's closure was the unanimous decision of a core group, I made it known to all the members when the decision was made and informed them if they had concerns or comments, they could come to me. After months of making sure everyone understood there was no defined leader among us, we came to the collective realization that naming one would be necessary to keep everyone moving forward and working efficiently. This was the first point in the development of the Kentucky 9/12 Project where I accepted responsibility for an action of the collective members, thus leaving me as the place where the "buck" now stopped. Rather than allow there to be any bickering or finger-pointing on decisions like these, I finally put my reluctance to lead aside and agreed to serve the group and its individual members in the best way I knew how. With great respect for the responsibility in front of me, I humbly accepted the designation of Director of the Kentucky 9/12 Project.

Perhaps this developmental milestone was also a turning point for the group. From that point forward, we worked hard to better define where we were headed, stayed more focused on our values and principles, and pushed back to the local groups and individuals to take more ownership and responsibility. We aimed at being a kind mother-figure encouraging our members instead of being a strict schoolmarm bossing our members. Rather than chasing hot button issues, we were focused again on ideas and values.

All of these decisions about the direction and focus of the group were made with the full knowledge that there would inevitably be consequences to follow. Yes, we lost a few initial members. We had people who told us that we would never keep going and would be nonexistent in months, but something else occurred. Trying to be one thing well as opposed to all things ordinary allowed people who believed as we did to reconnect with us and find common ground. Remarkably, our membership began to grow...as did the strength of the group.

Breakout

(noun) a forceful emergence from a restrictive condition or situation.

SEPTEMBER 2009

It had become overwhelmingly obvious by this point that our biggest obstacle was often a lack of clear direction for the group. We knew what we were standing against, and we were continually using education to reinforce those beliefs. Determining what we could do to make a difference in the world on behalf of those principles and values, though, was proving much more difficult.

Throughout the early portion of the development of our fledgling movement, some of what we had done was in large part simply satisfying the desires of our membership to be doing *something*. At this same time, though, there were continuously new people just waking up, and these new recruits were arriving with the fresh enthusiasm we had experienced in March. Now as the national political scene provided another huge trigger event in the health care legislation, there was an even larger influx of people. These folks all saw themselves as arriving at the start of a brand new movement. In many ways, this may have been a blessing in disguise for The 9/12 Project. It gave us a rare chance at hitting a reset button of sorts. We saw an opportunity to learn from our prior directional void and recreate the foundation of which we had previously lost sight.

During the initial 9/12 Project launch broadcast on March 13th, Glenn Beck told the viewing audience to save this date: Saturday, September 12th. This made logical sense as it was both the namesake of our group as well as a fundamental goal of our movement to bring Americans back to the people they were on September 12th, 2001. The day after America was attacked, we were not red states or blue states, not Republicans and Democrats, but united citizens.

Somewhere along the road to September 12th, a massive march on Washington, D.C. had been planned for this same date. As The 9/12 Project had been finding its way throughout 2009, there was also a larger and all-encompassing liberty movement that had been growing nationally. This march represented the opportunity for the liberty movement to flex its muscle on a national stage, and we were determined to be a part of it.

The event may not have been what we originally envisioned on March 13th, but that did not take away its importance to our members now. We were going, and we were going in a big way! This would be far and away our biggest leap of faith to date. It had been one thing to put on a seminar and potentially lose five hundred or one thousand dollars if absolutely no one showed up. It was quite another thing to put nearly twenty thousand dollars at risk if plans did not come together as we needed them to for any combination of reasons!

With six weeks remaining until we left and zero people registered for the trip to Washington, Lisa Williams swiped her personal credit card for over five thousand dollars on blind faith that we could do this. A few more weeks of prayer later, she put up another three thousand dollars. Finally, with only two weeks to go, we committed to a second bus, which meant another five thousand dollars out of our pocket. Lisa and I were literally on the phone every single day, checking the numbers, calculating our break-even point, and praying those last few seats or tickets would be sold. It was two days prior to our scheduled departure that we hit our break-even sale, and I was finally able to get my first full night's sleep in six weeks!

I should probably explain what all this money, stress, and planning were going toward. We were actually planning and coordinating several things that weekend. Our first order of business was arranging busses for people that wanted to make the ten-hour pilgrimage from Kentucky to Washington, D.C.

Yes, I said ten hours of bus riding. You can imagine what getting on a bus with fifty-four strangers and riding ten hours together might be like, I am sure. Well, it was nothing like that! Our journey began at 5:30am that Friday morning from a parking lot in Lexington, Kentucky where one hundred and ten people arrived ready to make the trip.

I stood in that dark parking lot behind a small folding table with a list of registered names while someone else stood over my shoulder holding a flashlight so I could read them. Another volunteer passed out gift bags that one of our members had put together for all the passengers. I thought I had all the important information about our trip in front of me in black and white, but it turned out that most of the truly important pieces of information were the things I did not yet know.

What I didn't know then was Jeff "Mario" Smith – who had made such an impression on me with his poem at the first tea party rally - was getting on that bus after many years of fighting against federal government expansion. He was a veteran and patriot who had fought for his country, but at this point he was feeling burned out, frustrated, and prepared to give up on the cause. Reluctantly, he had been talked into going on this trip and he was fully confident that it would be his last.

What I didn't know then was Ricky Hostetler was getting on that bus after having never been socially or politically active previously. He was a small business owner who was focused on what most self-employed entrepreneurs would worry about: his business. He had heard something about this bus trip, and made a spur-of-the-moment decision to buy tickets even though he had never attended any of our prior events or local meetings. He had no intention of becoming active, but felt that he just *had* to be a part of this outing.

When I boarded the bus, there were plenty of familiar faces looking back at me also. I saw the smiles of people who had become dear friends and who had shared their own personal motivations for making this trip with me. Susan Bennett, Jim and Niki Drake, Lisa Williams, as well as Jeff and Lisa Abler had been there with Lydia and I from the beginning, and they were all enthusiastic about the weekend that lay ahead of us in our nation's capital. There was another couple whose story I knew as that trip began, though I am still amazed by it today. Climbing aboard our bus were two inspiring patriots named Bob and Becky Pattie.

BOB & BECKY PATTIE

One month prior to our trip to D.C., I received a phone call from a gentleman named Bob asking me some questions about the trip. He was inquiring about what additional expenses there might be above the bus and hotel cost. In talking with him, it appeared he and his wife, Becky, were retired and on a fixed income. With recent unexpected expenses, they didn't know if they could afford the trip and were trying to budget down to the last penny. Next were some questions about how much walking there would be and if they could possibly get to the rally without having to walk. I assumed there might be some type of handicap involved and explained what I knew and said we would try to accommodate them. Finally, he said that they wanted to go but would need to get a doctor's release first. Becky had just gone through major heart surgery and they were not sure if she would be recovered by the time we were leaving. I was floored! They most likely couldn't really afford to go, but that was not going to stop them. Beyond that, his wife was in no condition to travel, but even that was a secondary concern to them. They felt that compelled with an urgent need - regardless of their obstacles - to make this trip. I got off that phone call with Bob Pattie, and I began to cry. This was why I was doing this; these were the people for which KY9/12 existed. It was not for the people that had themselves or their issue as their focus. It was not for my own publicity or for connecting with influential people. This was about the folks who nobody knew and had nothing to gain, but who felt in their hearts that they *had* to be a part of it. Bob and Becky Pattie represent the best of what The 9/12 Project can be, and why I devote my time to it. The story of their trip to Washington with us placed everything in perspective and — though they may never have known it - they were my inspiration and renewed energy to keep going.

We had new members that were just waking up to our movement that traveled hundreds of miles just to get on the bus that day. Like many of us had been back in March, these people arrived in our travelling party feeling frustrated, angry, and powerless. In the course of our ten-hour trip to Washington, they found out they were not alone, built relationships, and became determined. What I couldn't have possibly known then was that this bus trip would serve as an invaluable catalyst in helping a new crop of members bond with the core folks who had been together since our first event.

Some of my own thoughts on the bus ride, though, were unfortunately tinged with some personal sadness. Lydia was not able to attend with me as she stayed behind in Kentucky to care for our then two-month-old daughter Sophia. There were many mixed emotions inside both my wife and I during that Washington weekend. There was a feeling of disappointment. We started this journey together, and for the most part, we had worked in unison up to this point. Now with this first huge event being ten hours from home, I had to sadly go without her.

Even as the progress of the bus put hundreds of miles between us, I could sense the conflicted feelings with which Lydia must have been dealing. She had as much invested in our group as any of us, yet she was not on the trip. There must have been feelings of excitement and pride. She was glad for the group and thrilled that we were there on her behalf. She monitored the television news broadcasts, watched for any clips about the march, and called a dozen times to get updates from us. There was definitely a feeling of determination. Our new baby brought renewed focus to why we were making this march and why we were educating ourselves. We were working to ensure that this next generation could have a sustainable republic, and that they may understand where they came from and what would be required of them. Lydia knew we were there not only for her, but for our children – Aaron, Sarah, and little Sophia. There is no doubt that without her support, I would not have been there myself. Without her encouragement, I would not have been the driving force to organize this trip. In all likelihood, whether she knew it or not, without Lydia's support for me, KY9/12 may not have been represented in Washington at all that weekend.

Arranging the transportation for our Kentucky group was the easy part of our weekend planning. There was a much more complicated task waiting for us at the end of our bus ride. The Kentucky 9/12 Project was coordinating the first-ever national 9/12 Project reception on the evening before the march.

An understandable question at this point might be: how did Kentucky receive the honor of hosting the national 9/12 Project reception in Washington, D.C.? Quite simply, we didn't ask and just did it. Believe me when I say there was no arrogance motivating our group to take this on without being asked. It was truly pride in being 9/12ers. In truth, there were some misgivings among us that the spirit of The 9/12 Project - and its significance to us - was in some ways being overshadowed by the larger focus on the march itself. Each of us desired an opportunity to celebrate both who we were on this date and all that our efforts had made possible in the previous six months.

We had looked, listened, and hoped to hear of anything specifically planned for 9/12ers, but the weekend quickly approached with nothing to be found. With our new reaffirmed personal responsibility mantra, our group concluded that if something was going to happen, we may need to be the group to make it happen. Taking up the challenge head-on, we arranged a venue, ordered six thousand dollars' worth of appetizers, and began to organize the first-ever reception for 9/12ers from around the nation. I should have bought stock in antacid given the amount of heartburn that I experienced over this decision.

Our first outreach was to contact the chair of the national 9/12 Project, Yvonne Donnelly. I think she was as much surprised to hear from us as we were to quickly hear back from her! What better way to represent the national 9/12 Project than to have the national chairwoman speak? Additionally, we received confirmation that Rose Somma Tennent from the nationally syndicated morning radio program "The War Room with Quinn & Rose" agreed to speak at our event, as well.

All we needed now was for two hundred complete strangers from every corner of America to hear about our reception and find it enticing enough to buy tickets and fill the room. Thanks to the "Walk to Free Our Health Care" campaign that began in Kentucky but expanded nationwide, we had some contacts within other 9/12 groups around the country. These contacts, along with the help of Yvonne, and a mountain of e-mails to other groups, generated ticket sales that began to come in from everywhere. The reception sold out three days in advance, and the purchasers represented twenty-four different states and over thirty different 9/12 groups.

Though our Kentucky group had gotten the ball rolling on the reception, we received and accepted offers of assistance from around the country. The Florida 9/12ers were especially enthusiastic and helpful in volunteering their time and energy to make the event a success. One of the members from the Sunshine State even stepped up and sang a stirring rendition of the national anthem to open the night's festivities. The atmosphere in the room throughout the entire evening was nothing short of amazing. Two hundred people had walked through the doors not knowing what to expect from the event or the others in attendance, but the reception quickly took on the feel of a family reunion. Getting to experience that night of bonding with 9/12 members from across the nation, made our stressful weeks of planning completely worthwhile.

The wonderful reception experience served to further inspire and invigorate our Kentucky contingent. Even though the late night excitement had left us short on sleep, we were all up bright and early on the morning of September 12th. Our group set out to visit the Washington Monument and was soon flooded with emotions over the honor of walking together on such hallowed and historic ground. When we arrived, we discovered several 9/12 groups – as well as the smiling face of our national chair Yvonne – were also out enjoying each other's company and the beautiful morning on the National Mall. We were already feeling the solidarity and spirit of the day as we headed over to gather with hundreds of other groups at Freedom Plaza. It was hours before the march was scheduled to begin, and there was already an unfathomable sea of people that clogged the streets and sidewalks leading to the Capitol. From our location, we never heard an announcement or explanation from the platform, but with a little over an hour still remaining before the start of the march, people began to funnel their way down Pennsylvania Avenue.

It would be generous to describe the pace as a crawl given the mass of humanity in the streets. We had managed to keep about sixty KY9/12ers together to this point by three of us leading our little band's march with a Kentucky flag held above us and me manning a bullhorn. Much like some of our own events recently, at this point we had no idea where we were going or what we would do when we got there.

Upon arriving at the Capitol, the reality, or perhaps better said, the unreal truth of what we were now a part of came into view. We encountered not hundreds but hundreds of thousands of people. Our small group of sixty was thoroughly lost in this crowd, but that did not deter us. We wandered in and out through the crowd with our bullhorn in tow and willing KY9/12ers following close behind.

We ended up on a small patch of grass on the north side of the Capitol where we all made camp for the day. There were plenty of inconveniences and the lack of sleep to overcome, but no one allowed them to spoil the day for us. Port-a-potties were far outnumbered by the incredible lines of people seeking to use them, and the scarce food vendors were quickly sold out of everything. From our vantage point, we could not hear much and we definitely could not see anything. Yet for hours, we enjoyed the day, shared the experience with many new-found friends, cheered with the rest of the crowd, and joined in on the "U.S.A." chants. Never had any of us witnessed so many people with a common goal of liberty and restoring our republic.

In many ways, this was exactly the 9/12 spirit and it served as a great inspiration to keep the momentum going once we got back home. The enthusiasm was evident as we loaded the busses and headed back to Kentucky. The hours on the road were filled with in-depth discussions and idea-sharing conversations among the group that served to build strong and lasting relationships in our travelling party.

∽

FALL 2009

The successful completion of the reception and the trip was a milestone that I had been working toward for months. I had previously considered that achieving my personal goal of getting everyone to and from Washington, D.C. safe and sound might provide a logical end to my figurehead role in our group. Reaching that milestone, though, made it even clearer that my job was not yet complete and that the mission of KY9/12 was in many ways just beginning. For a portion of our group, the return from Washington served as their launching point. For many of the rest of us, this trip had served as further confirmation as to why we were coalescing around this common cause.

The next step we took as a group was to develop a core committee of members that became the executive board. These were the faces that had been there from the very beginning, understood the spirit of The 9/12 Project, and had been contributing factors in the prior progress of KY9/12. One of the key aspects, though, was that these people would join together, not as leaders, but fiduciaries of our refined mission and objectives.

Ironically, the first assembly of this new executive board was a meeting held in our home. Seven months after having to scrap plans to use our house for the viewing party due to the overwhelming response, we were now finally hosting a meeting thanks to the group's continued growth and success. That first board meeting was equal parts official business and celebration. The dinner table that Lydia and I shared every night with our family was now surrounded by the people who had become dear friends through our mutual devotion to a cause.

For the first time in our short history, the Kentucky 9/12 Project now had an executive board. We may not have had a physical office location or a full-time paid staff, but we had hard-working volunteers gathering in our homes and coordinating their efforts with the spirit of a family unit. We assumed we had everything we needed at that point. We still had the lingering excitement from our trip to Washington. We had a mission defined, goals set, and now on paper, we had our leadership team.

In the weeks and months that followed our inspirational journey to Washington, we had focused on trying to bring that energy of March 13th or September 12th back into each of our local community meeting events. We had seen the power that experiencing this energy firsthand had in turning new recruits into dedicated members. We had also seen the power that our local meetings had in building relationships among their regular attendees. We needed some way to energize local meetings into "mini-March 13th moments" to facilitate those bonding opportunities that truly engaged the assembled crowd and inspired them to continue participating.

In order to best explore our new ideas on how to empower our local meetings, we launched an initiative to find towns across Kentucky that did not have 9/12 groups and create one. Our highest priority for some time had been to start an active group in the state's largest city, Louisville. We had recently been contacted by an eager member in the area anxiously wanting to hold their first meeting. We instructed them to simply find-a venue, select a date, and we would handle the actual execution of the inaugural event.

Once the details were set, we sent hundreds of e-mails to members and others in the Louisville vicinity. I had planned to attend the meeting along with a couple of our other board members at a location described to us as an "Inn" near the airport. That sounded like a reasonable venue to us, so we set out for Louisville on the evening of the event.

In the days leading up to the meeting, I had been experiencing some pretty bad pain on my left side, and the strong pain medication rendered me unable to drive. Susan Bennett drove us over instead, and we made it into Louisville about an hour before the meeting was scheduled to begin. As we were following the directions we had been given, we drove by what looked from the outside like a biker bar of sorts on the same street as our venue. We were remarking that this street was an odd place for an inn when we realized that the biker bar was the inn. Wait a minute! This was our long-sought Louisville meeting location?

Not wanting to immediately judge a book by its cover, we went inside and...yeah, it was indeed a smoked-filled biker bar. We are talking about full "Road House" style here, too, with lights down really low and a stage fronted with chicken wire to stop the thrown bottles from hitting the performers. Now I have nothing against these sorts of watering holes, and the people there were very welcoming, but we had advertised this as a family-friendly local meeting. We were really looking for something a little less shocking for the kind of crowd we were anticipating. Like maybe someplace with overhead lighting?

Our all-too-familiar panic mode kicked in, and we quickly tried to find any alternatives within walking distance. We ended up at a Thai restaurant next door. I asked if they had any meeting rooms or something other than their main dining area, and they offered us their entire back room. The problem was that entire back room could hold a maximum of twenty people and we already had nearly twice that many people already milling around the biker bar and it was still half an hour until the meeting.

At last, we reluctantly returned to our original "Inn." They were kind enough to turn off the juke box and turn up the lights a little. That second part was probably not a great idea, because you could now see the less-than-ideal floors. Slightly embarrassed and slightly buzzed on pain medication, I spoke to over seventy-five people while standing behind chicken wire. Cross that crowning achievement off my bucket list!

This was not one of our shining moments by any means, but we struggled through. We managed to make it forty-five minutes until one of the bar patrons made his way to the middle of our crowd and shouted "you have talked enough…I want to hear some music!" Since I did not have any musical numbers planned for the evening, I took that heartfelt plea as my cue and quickly wrapped up the meeting from Hell and we headed back to Lexington.

Believe it or not, the seemingly disastrous atmosphere did not deter many of the people that came out that night. It was not about where we met, and with the speaker being medicated, I am quite sure it was not about what was said. Like so many of our activities, this was about people coming together, building bonds, and transforming anger into determination as a group.

I did not realize it then, but as it turned out, the unique Louisville meeting would be the best part of my evening. The raging pain I had been feeling for weeks finally reached its climax. By 3am, I found myself lying in the hospital being told I was facing emergency surgery. In retrospect, maybe I should not have made that trip to Louisville after all. Without warning and without time to plan, I was under the knife having six inches of my colon removed and extensive internal clean-up being performed.

I learned that I had acute diverticulitis, and it had only been the painkillers that had kept me going during the trip to Louisville. The diverticulitis ended up rupturing and causing my need for emergency surgery. Luckily, the rupture did not occur during the meeting, though that would have perhaps been the only thing that could have increased the absurdity of that scene!

The majority of the members in our group had no idea I even went through this ordeal. Even today, few know the severity of what I had or the strain it placed on my family and, to some extent, the KY9/12 executive board. I was completely out of service for seven weeks and our progress as a statewide group came to a screeching halt. There were no website updates and no e-mails going out.

The recovery from surgery provided me with some very much-needed down time for personal regrouping. For at least two weeks, I did absolutely nothing and took myself entirely out of the movement. I watched little or no news programming. I did not go on the internet at all. I wasn't on my cell phone or reading e-mails.

It was kind of nice, actually. It recharged my battery, but it also gave me better perspective by no longer being so enveloped in the day-to-day activities. The time away from everyone allowed me to see more clearly the truth that some of our activities were doing more to entertain our members than empower them. The flipside was the realization of the nearly limitless positive potential of continuing the educational focus of the group. Education about our nation's heritage of liberty and personal responsibility could serve as both the foundation for future generations and as enlightenment for the members of today.

All together, I spent almost two weeks in the hospital and an additional five weeks of recovery at home. Perhaps I should have spent this time in self-reflection, but I spent a good portion of it pondering the past, present, and future of KY9/12. Part of that mental evaluation included an immense sense of pride and joy that all our local groups had developed their own identities and leadership and were still going strong. Even though these scattered groups were operating in relative isolation from one another, their activity had not stopped just because I had.

On the other hand, the state KY9/12 website, the communication between groups, and everything we did at the statewide coordination level, had stopped cold during my absence. I realized then more than ever that empowering the local groups was the correct idea, and that we now needed more depth, empowerment, and structure at every level. It was no longer enough to have a leadership team on paper. We all needed a certain amount of empowerment and a better understanding of our roles. There was a balance that needed to be struck, and we were obviously not there yet.

As a group, we were now ready to take another step forward. Once I was recovered enough, we convened another executive board meeting to talk about who we wanted to be as a group, but we felt we needed to do more. We called an additional meeting, and we opened it up to all interested members. We invited anyone that had valuable perspectives to offer. Our desire for this meeting was to see new faces rise up that we could target to add to our executive board.

It was my firm belief after my surgery and recovery experience that we needed a broader base of members who felt empowered to take action – or even organize and lead action – when the necessary situations arose. In order to keep our group moving forward regardless of the inevitable bumps in the road ahead, we needed to have willing individuals aware of our unfulfilled needs and participation opportunities. Our initial attempt at encouraging this growth utilized the traditional approach of creating various committees and chairpersons and opening them up to our members.

We also unanimously decided on one word that clearly defined the mission we wanted to achieve: education. Now we just needed to understand what forms our pursuit of that mission would take. The year was quickly drawing to a close, so the time away from work around the holidays provided us all with a chance to reflect and brainstorm ideas for making our educational focus a priority in the coming year.

∽

JANUARY & FEBRUARY 2010

When 2010 arrived, our group was more organized than ever and had a strategic plan and purpose for our next activity. Our first initiative for the year was not focused on a random issue or prompted by the passion of a single member. Instead, we developed a somewhat complex and strategic series of projects with a single goal. For better or for worse, we had decided to tackle the issue of state sovereignty.

This was a somewhat logical decision given our state's heritage and the depth of educational opportunities it provided. Most of the 10th Amendment resolutions in other states that were getting attention could all trace their history to the first resolution penned by Thomas Jefferson. That very first state sovereignty resolution was signed in nearby Frankfort, Kentucky on November 10th, 1798. It was in response to President John Adams and the overreaching power created by the Alien and Sedition Acts passed earlier that year. In the summer after their passage, six thousand protestors – a massive crowd in those times - gathered in Lexington, Kentucky in opposition. Jefferson wrote the first resolution after that day, and it went on to the Kentucky House and passed by an overwhelming majority. This was the historic first line drawn in the sand between the federal government and states' rights and it lead to many other resolutions. It was our conviction that not only did "We the People" need to be reminded of these facts, but our elected officials needed constant reminding as well.

It was also a noble choice to focus our efforts on the 10th Amendment. All of the national problems that were in the headlines at that time could be traced back to this Amendment. Government-run health care was infringing on states' rights. Border security and illegal alien legislation was infringing on states' rights, Federal education standards and mandates were infringing on states' rights. With a strong 10th Amendment, we have a weaker federal government and a more powerful electorate. For those reasons alone, it was a noble cause to champion.

We had other reasons for aligning our group on this particular cause. Coming out of the holiday doldrums, we wanted to quickly focus everyone's energy and attention towards a single project. State sovereignty was an issue that could provide countless opportunities for local action, while being such a unifying belief for our members that everyone could easily galvanize around it.

Behind the scenes, we knew there was a growing frustration across not only our movement, but the national liberty movement at large, that we were not winning this battle overnight. As some members had been actively participating nonstop for nearly a year at this point, we were concerned they might soon reach burnout and wanted to provide everyone with a quick win and an invaluable opportunity to educate themselves on the workings of our state government. We believed we could swiftly bring about passage of a state sovereignty resolution in Kentucky given the political climate at the time. The people who chose to pour their time and energy into this effort would achieve a victory, and it would keep them motivated. That group accomplishment would create a bond for those that went through the process together and further empower them to believe they could do anything. The plan was equal parts history, sociology, psychology, and political science.

This initiative was a planned series of projects and not just a one-time event. We organized a petition and traveled the state gathering signatures. This personalized the experience for the people that chose to sign and allowed them to feel like they were part of this fight with us. We had coordinated phone-calling and letter-writing campaigns that gave participants a true feeling of taking action, while confirming the perception of conflict between legislators who did not support the resolution and the will of the people. We held rallies so the crowds could see they were all in it together and not alone in this fight.

We also empowered people to begin doing things on their own towards this cause. We organized a committee of members with a passion for this issue to focus especially on it, and we gave them full discretion to send out e-mails and hold rallies of their own. All their work - when combined with our structured plan of attack - gave the overwhelming impression to our membership that we were gaining momentum and that they were on a winning team regardless of the State Sovereignty Resolution's eventual outcome.

One of our most-discussed member-initiated actions was something they called "Sovereignty Stampedes." The idea was nothing short of fantastic. We would encourage people to go to the state capital on the day the committee was hearing the resolution and simply exercise their right as a citizen to sit in on the committee meeting while wearing large 10th Amendment buttons on their chests.

Sovereignty Stampede

Event Details

The time has come for us to take action on our State Sovereignty! It has become apparent that the majority of our legislators are not listening. Phone calls, e-mails, and personal visits have not swayed anyone to give HCR 10 (State Sovereignty Resolutions) a hearing. We must show numbers in Frankfort on the same day.

KENTUCKY KNOWS BEST PAC

When
Tuesday, March 9, 2010 7:30am (ET)

Where
Capitol Building 700 Capitol Ave

57 KY9/12ers are going

I know as frustrating and tempting as it may be please no Pitchforks or torches....

What we as a group, nor the folks at the capital, ever anticipated was sixty people taking the day off from work and making the trip to do as we had asked. As it turned out, the committee room could only hold about ten spectators. When faced with sixty people anxious to hear their discussion, the committee chairman who was opposed to our resolution decided he was not up for this publicity and canceled the meeting.

The folks who had made personal sacrifices to be there on a workday did not like this response, so we now had five dozen upset patriots going through the halls of the capital looking for anyone to give them answers. If the goal of the opposed chairman was to avoid publicity, he failed miserably on this one. Things certainly would have gone smoother if he had just held the meeting as planned. Instead, he literally played an impromptu game of hide-and-seek before calling police officers in for protection from a group made up in large part of senior adults and children. The entirely comical situation made for much more publicity of their determination to ignore the citizens than anything we could have done on our own. Not to mention that video of the entire ordeal made for fantastic viewing on YouTube!

At last, the issue came to a climax and even went a little too far. The last attempt to force a vote on the State Sovereignty Resolution happened with just a couple of weeks remaining before the end of the legislative session. By this point, the supporters had gone through a great deal just to get that far and there would be no backing down now. With just a single day's notice to the group and with most of us working full-time jobs, an amazing contingent of 9/12ers managed to show up for no other purpose than to sit quietly in a balcony viewing gallery and watch the proceedings. We were not permitted to talk or even applaud, but we were an impressive physical presence.

This sizable showing was totally unprecedented for any prior issue and the politicians on the floor below clearly did not know what to think or expect. Apparently, they assumed the worst of us. Having been alerted by the politicians below and seemingly ready for some sort of conflict, the capital police were visibly on edge when they appeared in the balcony around us.

An over-reaction of the part of the capital police soon confirmed that the situation had gone too far. The officers interpreted it as a threat when a member of our group - who was sitting on the steps talking to the person in the adjacent seat - would not immediately take a seat when instructed by them. There was some slight physical contact, followed by confusion, concluding with our member on the receiving end of a taser. The man was led away by police and then, after recovering, released without any consideration for any charges. Once again, what could have been a quiet day with sixty people sitting and observing state government in action turned into a scene that furthered incited ordinary citizens against their unresponsive government and for the State Sovereignty Resolution.

Sadly, after months of diligent hard work, our efforts came up short. The State Sovereignty Resolution never even came to a vote in the Kentucky State House of Representatives due to some political technicalities. In these months, we had people signing petitions, sending letters, making calls, coming out to rallies, educating themselves, and becoming activists. We did get more people involved with their state government affairs, and many of those people walked away from this experience feeling more empowered and determined than ever before.

The problem now became that, without a clear victory to rally around and provide a stronger foundation to build from, we were only as good as the next big initiative we would pursue. We were heading into March, and with primary election season about to be in full swing, political campaigns were the clear hot social issue. Having taken a hard stance to define our group as non-partisan and education-focused, we did not exactly fit in that world. While we may not have yet had the next big event planned for ourselves, what we did have was a recognized group, a good number of active members, and a lively movement...if we could keep it.

Coalescense

(noun) the union of diverse things into one body or form or group.

MARCH 2010

We continued reaching out to members outside of the executive board for advice and help with steering the group as a whole. The process had worked well initially, but by this point we had the same people showing up each month and were faced with continually hearing new versions of the same ideas being repeated. My curiosity led me to wonder if a few hand-picked people had been good for us, might a lot more people that we didn't know from Adam be even better.

This theory set the stage for our next advisory meeting. A call went out for any interested parties to attend, and the executive board members were encouraged to each invite someone from outside the group completely to join us. The resulting meeting featured over one-third of the attendees consisting of individuals that were not even members of KY9/12. While this may have been a perfect formula for chaos, one decidedly good thing came from it.

As we had just concluded our State Sovereignty initiative and had grown to better understand where we best fit as a group, we began to discuss what was next for us. For the first time as an assembled group, we were talking strategically about our focus on education. Perhaps predictably, we began talking ourselves in circles to some degree about assorted things we had done in the past or could potentially do in the future. This point in the conversation is when a question was asked by one of the people in attendance who was not a member of the group and that no one seemed to even know.

"So...what exactly are you guys wanting to accomplish?" It was a fair question, and we attempted to answer with a standard vague sound bite response like "make government smaller and 'We The People' stronger."

"Okay...but what does that mean?" This was also a fair question that deserved a good response. A response the likes of which I am sure I did not provide, because the gentleman quickly expanded on his reply which consisted primarily of informing us that our group seemed to him like a complete waste with no purpose.

Being backed in a corner now, I did what most people do and retreated to my comfort zone of what I did know about our group. I jumped up on my soapbox and launched into who we were as people. Common citizens coming together to see they were not alone, being based on a core set of proven principles and values that helped form this nation, having heritage-based education and enlightenment as our focus, and striving to empower people to act based on the foundation we provided.

While the meeting clearly did not go well exactly, what did come from it was the exposure of an obvious question that we had yet to answer. Our inability to provide a good answer to that question haunted me for days, and I think it forced our entire group to resolve to come up with a response. We understood that the response needed to be a logical extension of the form our group had already taken and desired to retain.

It had been one year since our founding, and the same reasons that brought us together then still rang true twelve months later. Sure, our activities had been all over the board with some hits and some misses. What had never changed was our foundation of nine principles, twelve values, bringing like-minded people together, promoting personal responsibility, and encouraging education.

Now having more time to filter that frustrated gentleman's question through those foundational beliefs, our eyes were opened to what our answer needed to be. What did the Kentucky 9/12 Project hope to accomplish? We desired to inspire individuals and groups to connect with their communities through education, service, and dedication to our 9 Principles and 12 Values. Beyond that, we realized more than ever that the key was education. Acting on emotion, you can get people to react and effect temporary changes, but through providing knowledge and information, you can create lasting generational changes.

We had learned a lot of lessons as a group, but it was still hard to believe that nearly a full year had passed since our humble beginnings. I could not help but reminisce about all the wonderful people I had been blessed to meet in those twelve months. Many of the acquaintances I had made during the trip to Washington had blossomed into treasured friendships. I was exchanging regular e-mails and phone calls with other state leaders, as well as keeping in touch with Yvonne about the national direction of The 9/12 Project. Our excitement was building as we were just one week away from the first anniversary of the original Glenn Beck viewing party that launched our grassroots movement. That week, my phone rang and when I answered, the lady on the line introduced herself as a producer for the Glenn Beck program.

Okay...she had my full attention now!

They were putting together an anniversary special to air on March 12th and wanted me as a guest on the program. I was shocked at the opportunity, but equally humbled and honored to represent our Kentucky 9/12 Project. Making an appearance on Glenn's television show would alter the way I was perceived as a leader within our state group also. Seeing my face on national television after having received countless e-mail messages from me over the past year, would legitimize my position with the devoted Glenn Beck fans in our membership. This exposure would make it so that - even if I wanted to — it would be nearly impossible to disassociate myself from our cause or my role in it anytime soon.

I was flown out to New York City on a Thursday to tape the show for a Friday night broadcast, and the entire experience was surreal for me. It was a whirlwind that found me sitting in a town car from the airport, sitting in the green room, sitting in a make-up chair, and finally sitting on stage with Glenn Beck facing multiple cameras. My segment was admittedly brief and added very little content to the overall program, but every second of it was an honor. I was joined on the panel that day by 9/12ers from Florida, New York, and Ohio, as well as Yvonne representing our national organization. Together with Glenn, we discussed and celebrated all that our groups had accomplished in our first year of existence, as well as the things we were working on for the future. Being a part of the anniversary of The 9/12 Project, and being there as a representative of what everyone in Kentucky had experienced and accomplished in the past year, was the experience of a lifetime.

This whole New York outing, as well as everything I had done for the prior year, was perhaps best captured not during my moments on the show, but as I was flying home. Answering questions from Glenn Beck on national television is one thing, but the most difficult question I received that weekend was on the plane ride home. It came in the form of the most clichéd traveling query of them all.

Sitting beside a stereotypical-looking businessman, he asked if I was in New York for business or pleasure. Rather than dismissing the question with the polite chit-chat that he no doubt expected, I paused and realized neither option was really applicable to me. How would he react if I said "neither?"

The 9/12 Project was not "business." It was not how I made my living. I was not receiving any paychecks for the time and sacrifice it had required of my family and of me. It was not what I had any prior training in my life to do.

The 9/12 Project was not "pleasure." It was not what I most wanted to be doing at this stage of my life. I had a wonderful wife, a nine-month-old baby, and two great pre-teen kids that I could be enjoying time with at home. It was not my hobby or something one could just tinker around with on the weekends.

The 9/12 Project took hours of our time every week. We chose to do it in response to our firm belief that our nation – our republic - was in such grave danger it demanded we do something. We did this because we had to; we did this for survival. So you tell us: was The 9/12 Project business or pleasure?

‿

SPRING 2010

By April, we had come a long way and really defined some key areas of focus as well as some key things we hoped for our group to avoid. With education as our mantra, we started getting back to the basics and once again focused on encouraging people to get together locally and start meeting in their own communities. Seeing as I had just returned from New York as a bit of a newly-minted "celebrity" in Kentucky, we used this window of opportunity for me to call people to action on behalf of the KY9/12 Project's cause.

We had started with four local groups that held meetings right after the initial viewing party, and just over one year later, we had ten local meetings planned around the state of Kentucky every month. Each local group was an individual movement unto themselves, shaping the dialogues in their community and the unique direction of their group. I went to many of these meetings and used my eighty-six seconds of Glenn Beck fame to reinforce to each group what The 9/12 Project was and to visibly show my support for each of the local group leaders. We were not telling anyone how to run their meetings or what they could or could not do, but there was an unspoken collective identity and overall movement culture around 9/12ers that was always present.

In essence, what we had now was a brand, and these groups - and other groups still to come - had the freedom to embrace and represent that brand in their communities. At the same time, I was actively promoting the brand of KY9/12 on the Glenn Beck program, in newspapers, local radio interviews, and through e-mails and website communications. We had our principles and values to unite the group and defined leaders to coordinate and promote the group. At the same time, our individual members and local units were continually encouraged and empowered to take action on their own as they saw fit.

The key for us remained finding ways to build upon our education focus. The local groups really picked this effort up and began to promote heritage-based educational topics by bringing in historians, professors, and other speakers with expertise in areas of interest to their members. This education component infused our folks with a desire to reignite passion for history in people both inside and outside our group and that made us stand out from the many other liberty groups active in our state.

At the statewide level, we looked to provide other large-scale opportunities for education to our members as well. We brought back the National Center for Constitutional Studies and held three more "Making of America" seminars around the state. Instead of just passing out pocket Constitutions, which seemed to be a symbolic or popular thing to do in those days, we began passing out copies of "The 5000 Year Leap." The posts on our website became noticeably less about issues and calls for action and more about providing links where people could become informed and stay alert on their own.

We also planned and staged a three-day tour across Kentucky featuring the nationally-recognized organization "American Majority." Beka Romm, one of their talented presenters, did a fantastic seminar called "The System" explaining how as a nation we got to where we were and some steps we could take going forward. We also provided information to our local groups about available speakers with some particular expertise on topics ranging from the "Faith of our Founding Fathers," to history and facts about global economies, to the 17th Amendment, and various other topics.

We were enlightening, educating, and empowering. We were slowly shifting from simply reacting to current events and acting out of emotions to educating ourselves and empowering people to protect and restore the things we loved most about our country. It is a corny way to explain, but instead of leading people to a pond and catching them some fish, we were teaching them how to fish and allowing them to find their own fishing holes.

Our focus on education also helped us distinguish ourselves from the other groups and activities that did not share our priorities and purpose. April 15th represented an anniversary date for all those commemorating the first large round of nationwide tea parties on

Tax Day 2009. Recalling our history with those inaugural tea parties, we had prominently promoted, supported, and even played a role in planning a few events.

For the Tax Day rallies of 2010, though, we subtly posted a listing on our message board with contact information for the various event organizers. We did not promote any specific events with e-mail communications or website banners. Personally, I turned down two speaking opportunities, and due to scheduling conflicts, did not even have an opportunity to attend any rallies on April 15th itself. We were not downplaying the effectiveness of importance of these rallies – just the role of The 9/12 Project in them.

Our members were encouraged to support rallies in their area on their own, as we felt a strong importance for these tea parties to take place and be well-attended for the sake of the larger liberty movement. What we also knew, though, was that many of these tea parties had grown strong enough in the prior year that we would only be duplicating their efforts in many ways. Many of our members were supporters or active in multiple liberty groups, and they had the personal responsibility and opportunity to participate on their own.

The bottom line, though, was that we were not a tea party group. While they were perhaps issue-and-candidate-oriented, we were principle-focused. While they were protest-or-activist-oriented, we were focusing on educating ourselves and others. While they hoped to be an influence in changing public policies, we were hoping to be an influence in changing people's mindsets. While they tried to gather large numbers together as a sign of opposition, we were encouraging members to gather in small groups to find support. Of course, not actively promoting these rallies did draw some criticism, but April 16th arrived with no serious consequences.

If we thought we ruffled feathers with tea party organizers by not promoting their events as vigorously as they would have liked, we had an even bigger backlash coming from our handling of the political candidates in the coming election. While we were having regular discussions as a group about how to best utilize our non-partisan, education-focused stance to serve our members during the campaign and election season, we were regularly receiving some strongly-worded guidance from the political establishment.

"This is the most important election ever, and you must endorse candidates to make sure we get the right people in office and we win the Senate and House."

"The only way we can achieve our goals is through numbers at the ballot box this year."

"I mean…you can do education all day long, but if we don't win this year, and you don't tell people who to vote for, there won't be a future!"

We respectfully disagreed.

What about personal responsibility? Should we not encourage members to educate themselves about the candidates and cast the best possible votes for themselves and their families? Did we have the arrogance to believe our group's endorsement would persuade someone to vote a certain way? Would a person who made up their mind based on what some group said without researching for themselves not be practicing the exact type of ignorance that we were fighting against?

One particular campaign manager went as far as informing me that it would be my fault if his candidate lost because our group did not send people to make phone calls or walk door-to-door on his behalf. I responded by asking him why he was not calling and blaming the local VFW for a potential defeat. What was the difference between that non-partisan group and ours? We did not have the responsibility or desire to be an extension of any party. If he was the campaign manager, it was his job - or even more the candidate's responsibility - to win this election as well as their own fault should they lose.

We were combating this ignorance by educating people on where they came from, where they needed to go, and providing them with a set of principles and values to filter that information. Despite the hyperbole being thrown at us, our group realized that this was not the most important election in our lifetime. While this election would affect the balance of our current republic, the longer-lasting fight for individual liberty would require an informed electorate. The lesser of two evils is still evil, and replacing one letter (D) with another letter (R) would not fix this problem.

People might be angry at those in office, but just going out and finding another angry man or woman to replace them will not solve the problem. We were beyond parties and elections, and there was a fundamental issue with our citizenry that needed to be righted before this country could get back on the right track. With that guiding belief, we concentrated on the people more than the candidates that lobbied for our support. We were focused on personal responsibility and grounding everyone in our principles and values to allow each individual to find and vote their own conscience. This would ensure the continued prosperity or our nation rather than a single political win.

We were proud of our non-partisan designation and believed that both major parties contributed equally to the country's current problems. At the same time, we didn't support a third party alternative as the better solution either. Instead, we extol the Founding Fathers' championing of the individual citizen and believe that any politician with honor and conviction of principles - regardless of party affiliation - will protect and preserve the Constitution.

Our political stance became more of a challenge, but we wore it as our badge of honor. I think every major candidate in our area asked me to lunch - not because they liked me so much - as they were courting support from the Kentucky 9/12 Project. Never one to pass up a free lunch, I would meet them but never had the heart to tell them that I was trying so hard to be unbiased that I was even afraid to put a sign in my front yard for fear that someone would connect it to a transferred endorsement from KY9/12. This was perhaps – okay, definitely - going overboard, but it was important at the top of this new organization that we remained non-partisan. While on the local level, groups did provide forums for many of them to speak; we would never give any implied endorsement from the group itself. This balancing act was never easy. We had some really great candidates - who believed in many of our core values- that I personally supported, but we stuck to our principles and stance of not publicly supporting or endorsing anyone.

When I mention really great candidates, that list includes local 9/12ers that stepped up and threw their hats into the ring for office. I had encouraged everyone that the liberty movement was a participatory sport and they needed to get involved and even consider running for office. A few folks actually took me seriously, and I could not have been happier for them. These brave souls stepped up to take on the establishment and status quo for a chance to use the principles and values they now had as their foundation in public service. They made us all proud as they embraced personal responsibility and never ran as "9/12ers" but as patriotic citizens and principled candidates.

While we maintained our position of not endorsing any campaigns – even those of our own members - we did want to provide our members with access to the primary participants and allow them to come to their own conclusions. The suggestion was made that we could potentially host a debate, and we eventually decided to try. Our final decision was based on a couple of factors. First, the debate would accomplish our goal to provide a fair and equitable forum to meet the candidates. Second, the debate would generate cool and widespread publicity for our group. We opted to host a primary debate for the United States Senate race. Making our choice more interesting was the intense national attention on that particular race with the liberty movement favorite Rand Paul running against the current Kentucky Secretary of State Trey Grayson in the Republican primary.

Leading our efforts was Rita Ramsay, a dedicated member who had *zero* experience at staging an event like this before, but - in the 9/12 spirit - didn't let that stop her. We set a date, then changed the date, then talked to one of the candidates and changed the date again, and then heard from another candidate requesting a date change. Yes, I think we went through six different dates before landing on one that all the candidates could agree to, and even then we had some issues.

Wanting to do things just a little differently, we decided to go with a less-traditional Rick Warren-style interview forum where the candidates would receive the same questions separately in two individual segments. Making it a true 9/12 effort, we asked members to submit their own questions and then narrowed them down to a final list of twelve. Over one hundred quality questions came in across a wide range of topics. I would have to say - and heard others agree - that our twelve questions were the best ones that these candidates would face in the entire campaign. Everything was coming together perfectly.

When the endlessly rescheduled date finally arrived, we converged on a local high school auditorium for the debate. As the program got underway, there were little hiccups that we had to overcome. I was frustrated that the sound and lighting we were paying for did not perform well for either candidate's portion of the show. The wireless microphones had issues and the lighting created bad shadows for our video recording. Even with all that said, I gave the event five stars, and had never been more proud or satisfied with our results. Thanks to the incredible organizational efforts of Rita Ramsay, everything we had hoped for, we accomplished.

I did not see any forum during the entire primary season that compared to our truly fair and unbiased showcase for the candidates. Our debate highlighted strengths, exposed questionable stances, and did not allow anyone to escape to the normal talking points or stump speeches they had rehearsed. We had two hundred people that raved about the event and walked away satisfied. The best compliment I received was from a woman on her way out the door with buttons for both candidates on her jacket. She told me that she went in the auditorium not knowing who she would vote for and - thanks to our debate - she could now confidently make an informed decision. She then proceeded to remove one of the buttons before continuing on her way. The debate also accomplished our selfish goal of being a cool experience that generated excellent publicity for our group's efforts and went further to legitimize us in our community.

The primary campaigns finally ended, the elections were held, and the winners prevailed. While everyone heard plenty about Rand Paul and the "Tea Party" victories, there were many other patriots that may not have been recognized who were liberty-driven and principles-focused candidates. Among these were some personal friends, 9/12ers, and people who took the chance and responsibility on their own to try to become a representative of the people. These were not always the individuals who attended rallies as a speaker or organizer, but rather the faces in the crowd waving their "Don't Tread on Me" flags. Their motivation to run was not a political calculation but was instead an answer to that inner voice calling them to do what was right for themselves, their families, and their nation.

Shortly after the September 12th trip to Washington, D.C., Ricky Hostetler decided to run for a seat in the Kentucky House of Representatives. Standing in that crowd of a million people had personalized this movement for him, and he resolved that he needed to do whatever he could. He had never considered running for office before and prayerfully weighed the potential consequences of ultimately deciding to put himself - and more significantly his family - through an election. His eventual choice to run was inspired by his passion for our state and our nation – not by his personal political aspirations.

Ricky found himself in a contested Republican primary against a candidate who had been groomed for a run at the House seat by the party establishment. He was no longer just a bystander, but was actually running against the will of the top brass in his own party. As he was facing not only his opponent but well-connected insiders, he was easily out-spent during the campaign. He did not know anything about the art of politicking and had no political strategists to advise him. He would have to overcome his lack of resources by building relationships and focusing on values. For five months straight, he went out knocking on one door at a time to personally request each voter's support. He stood strong in his beliefs, wore his heart on his sleeve, did things the only way he knew how, and made his family and all of us very proud in the process.

On Election Day, Ricky Hostetler unfortunately lost his bid to represent the 62nd district in which he and I lived by a very slim margin. It would not ring true to say his dream came to an end because this had never been about fulfilling a personal dream. It would also be wrong to consider his loss as a setback for the greater liberty movement. While the established party candidate might have won, an average electrician had decided to wake up, get active, attempt to do something about our state's problems, and run for office to help end the practice of politics as usual. This is a testament to our cause and the spirit of our movement. The ordinary men and women fighting in small towns across the country to defend our individual voices and personal liberties embody the essence of The 9/12 Project.

෬

SUMMER 2010

One of the most pleasant surprises we received along our journey came in the form of a local meeting group that started without any prompting from us or even any initial connection with The 9/12 Project. They called their group the Owensboro Liberty Book Club, and its founding members shared our commitment to principles and values as well as our drive for self-education. They met weekly and as a group went systematically through many liberty books like "The 5000 Year Leap" and "The Federalist Papers" and had in-depth discussions about them. Those regular conversations amongst their members produced some very good ideas as well.

While talking to their organizer about upcoming meetings, he mentioned an idea that one person had shared of starting a "Vacation Liberty School." That was all I needed to hear. I immediately realized this concept was perfect. It was exactly what we were about: reaching out to the public and providing heritage-based education. It was laying a foundation with our youth to provide the next generation with long-lasting liberties, and it facilitated a principled approach to help find and cultivate the next George Washington.

We tinkered with their original concept slightly and envisioned a week-long program - running for a couple of hours every evening - geared toward middle school-aged kids. It would be modeled after the familiar "Vacation Bible School" church programs, but with a focus on our principles, our heritage, and aspects of faith and how it influenced the Founding Fathers and our nation. Within a few days, I had sent out some "feelers" to people, and I was receiving amazing feedback. If all of our gut instincts were right, this was looking like a big idea.

Days later, at our next executive board meeting, I not only presented the idea, but hand-picked one of our board members that I thought would be perfect for this project. Lisa Abler listened to the idea with mixed emotions. I could tell that she, too, understood what we had and what potential there was for it. At the same time, she saw how overwhelming it would be and wondered how it would fit her already hectic life.

She prayed about it, and soon her and her husband, Jeff, took it on with the same passion they had shown with so many of our other activities in the past. What we were asking out of them now, though, would be a much larger challenge. It was the second week of June when they began working, and they had just three weeks to produce a complete curriculum for a week-long VLS.

Our entire group was confident that no couple could have been better suited for this project. While they were not entrepreneurs in the traditional sense of having started their own business, they had that unmistakable spirit in them. They took on this challenge, did what needed to be done, and never questioned their own ability to achieve it. They knew how to take an idea, put their inherent talents and initiative into action, and make it a reality.

LISA & JEFF ABLER

Of all the values of The 9/12 Project, the one that comes to mind first when I think of Lisa and Jeff Abler is easily personal responsibility. Lisa was already well-informed and empowered before The 9/12 Project began. She has a master's degree in microbiology and made the decision to be a *true* stay-at-home mom and home-school their three children, allowing them to benefit from her influence and abilities. She never viewed this decision as a personal sacrifice, but instead saw it as the best option for her to fulfill her responsibility to her children as a mother. Jeff is an engineer by trade who is more comfortable using critical thinking to solve problems than standing in front of a group and facilitating meetings. He would have never pictured himself leading monthly local group meetings, but he clearly saw how important these roles would be to the future success of The 9/12 Project. He volunteered and became the local group coordinator for his city. When we all first assembled on March 13th, they were frustrated like many of us, but they felt a responsibility to join and support a larger group that shared their beliefs. They understood the power of bonding together, and just knew that they needed to be there that day. From that first meeting on, Lisa and Jeff have continually been there for the Kentucky 9/12 Project, willing to step out of their comfort zones, take time away from their other responsibilities or interests, and doing whatever needs to be done.

It was amazing what Lisa and Jeff accomplished in the time they were given. The success or failure of Vacation Liberty School was going to rest squarely on the two of them, and they were determined to see it succeed. Being a homeschooling household, they approached the development of material for VLS with much the same process they used to put together curriculum for their own kids. They began by deciding what they wanted the students to learn and then applied their past experience to identify the most effective way for them to grasp and retain those concepts. Our goal was for children to learn our fundamental principles and values, and the best scenario would be for each child to discover them firsthand by experiencing them at some level.

The purpose of Vacation Liberty School was clear. Regrettably, there has been a void in public education and understanding plaguing recent generations of Americans pertaining to the values on which our country was founded. History has slowly been changed to be more "politically correct" and rewritten to fit a misguided agenda. The mission of VLS was to educate, enlighten, and excite the youth of America about the beliefs, fundamentals, and principles on which this country was founded and to empower them with the knowledge and will to preserve these ideas and liberties for our nation. We would instill pride in faith, the Founding Fathers, and this nation through a blend of activities, games, skits, and teaching. The concepts and ideas were simple, but the results – if we were successful - could prove to be profound.

After a couple of weeks filled with intense rounds of curriculum conception, structuring, and rough documentation came a furious scramble to complete all the necessary implementation planning as well as buying or building from scratch everything that was needed. After little sleep and much prayer, the Ablers made some final adjustments and were ready to test the VLS concept. In order to work out as many of the kinks as possible, their first audience would be a small pilot program comprised of the children of 9/12ers, including our own kids - Sarah and Aaron.

The volunteer staff involved in staging the original program was typical of the diverse backgrounds that can always be found in a 9/12 organization. Among the team were an engineer, artist, data analyst, homeschooling mom, microbiologist, electrical contractor, insurance agent, Gulf War veteran, and my wife Lydia. Though they represented a wide spectrum of life experiences and fields of wisdom, the group was united by a common passion for our great nation and seeing liberty thrive throughout future generations.

Early in the week-long pilot program, we realized that it was the unique personalities and tremendous talents of our volunteers that would truly make VLS special and fun for the children. The ideas, observations, and experiences of the staff combined with the comments from the kids provided the final enhancements for the maturing content. We launched a website featuring the detailed curriculum that would have made any educator proud but remained simple enough for any 9/12 group to digest and use for themselves. It explained the programs and games for the kids as well as provided instructions and suggestions for the props they had created. Lisa and Jeff Abler had led the way on taking an idea from the Owensboro Liberty Book Club all the way through to implementation as a fully-developed community outreach tool for 9/12 Project groups across the nation to utilize.

Now it was time to open the flood gates! The first official week of education aimed to help introduce kids to our fundamental principles and values was underway. As the kids arrived, their first encounter was me — donning a three-cornered hat and colonial vest - posing as the tyrannical king's servant. In a matter-of-fact voice, I commanded each new subject where they were to sit and repeated the rules they must follow while in the "Old World." As I began to lead a never-ending chorus of "Twinkle Twinkle Little Star," the kids soon surmised that a preferable environment might be found beyond the floor-to-ceiling black sheets separating them from the rest of the room. First, one bold child ventured out, and then increasing groups of them left and navigated through a maze to the "New World."

The week went by with the kids - referred to as "colonists" during VLS - playing more games, earning "gold nugget" candies, and spending them in a general store. They got to hear from Martha Washington and re-live Reverend Thomas Price's famous sermon and prayer from the Old South Church in Boston. Using illustrations from history, the quotes of our Founding Fathers, and clever games and scenarios designed by the Ablers, the kids enjoyed the week and were able to comprehend the consequences of too much or too little governmental control of personal freedoms. After the week was over, we had laid a foundation of principles and values and, quite possibly, planted the seed for the next George Washington to grow.

Vacation Liberty School

Event Details

It use to mean something to tell your children they could grow up and become President. Now we need more; we need the next George Washington. We have been educating ourselves and becoming active for our children and grand children's sake but have we given them the tools and foundation to keep the light of liberty burning. We believe it is through education, a deep knowledge of our American heritage, and a foundation of faith, is the only way that liberty will survive and thrive.

With the children there will absolutely be no Pitchforks or torches....

When

Monday, July 12, 2010 6:00pm (ET)

Where

Gano Church   212 Bevins Lane

130 KY9/12ers are going

For over a year, we had talked of making education a priority for the sake of the next generation of patriots, and now we had finally produced an outlet to present our timeless principles and values to that generation directly. The positive feedback that we received from the students and their parents was enough to bring tears to our eyes. They were as grateful to our group for offering the program as we were to them for taking a step of faith and participating in such a new concept.

What we were doing in Kentucky did not go unnoticed. First, the Associated Press did a story on it, which was picked up by over three hundred newspapers and read on air by Glenn Beck during his radio program. The story of VLS highlighted a great accomplishment for our Kentucky group, but more importantly, the end result was a program that illustrated everything The 9/12 Project was about. Turned out, that is exactly what Glenn Beck said on his radio program on that July 15th, a moment that most of us will not soon forget...

GLENN: *Try this story. This is out of Kentucky. This is in the Associated Press: "Call it vacation Bible School Beck-style. Some three dozen kids ages 10 to 15 are spending five nights this week learning what organizers, some with tea party ties, say they won't hear in school about the Constitution, Founding Fathers and the role of faith and the birth of the United States. 'If we're going to take our country back, we've got to remember where we came from. Not only as adults, but we need to teach our children,' said Tim Fairfield, one of the teachers who wore a three-cornered hat at the opening class at Vacation Liberty School. It's held in a church basement in Georgetown, Kentucky, a city just north of Lexington. It is the site of two major Toyota assembly plants. The curriculum includes lessons like equal rights, not equal results. Recognize men, don't — one class is recognize that men don't create rights; God creates rights, and understanding falsehoods of separation of church and state. Organizers say the program has drawn interest from people looking to start new chapters in Ohio, Colorado, New York, Florida, and other communities in Kentucky."*

Thank you. As a citizen, thank you. (Glenn begins to cry) *This isn't anyone else's country; this isn't anyone else's responsibility. This is the individual's responsibility. You will be the key. If we remember who we are, we will be able to preserve it in one form or another so it is not lost from the face of the Earth. But we will also grow the next generation. We have a chance if we just remember the truth and restore those truths and live our lives with honor. Thank you. Thank you, thank you, 9/12 Project members, I pray for you every night. Thank you."*

It is hard for me to describe the emotional impact that hearing this on the radio had on the members of our group. The segment brought many of us to tears, as Glenn got choked up himself. Receiving recognition from the person who had launched The 9/12 Project was nice, but it was far more important and rewarding that he clearly grasped the significance and motivation for our work. He also confirmed what we already knew. Vacation Liberty School was the epitome of what The 9/12 Project was all about, and was exactly the approach we needed to be taking. Remarkably, Lisa and Jeff Abler's hard work delivered it at exactly the right time.

From that moment forward, it got even crazier. I received my second phone call from producers of the Glenn Beck television program. As much as I might have been tempted to expand upon my eighty-six seconds of broadcast glory, this time it was Lisa's turn to enjoy the experience, and it was something she had clearly earned. The next week, Lisa was flying to New York, where Vacation Liberty School was highlighted and she was introduced as an "Everyday American Hero." As a result, traffic to the VLS website skyrocketed and other 9/12 groups and like-minded liberty groups from around the country began e-mailing with questions and comments about organizing their own local Vacation Liberty Schools.

Whereas Ed - the caller from Connecticut – and his emotional plea had served as a catalyst to the creation of The 9/12 Project, VLS may serve as that same catalyst to our future as a movement. This creative - and easily reproducible - learning environment could prove to be the most important thing we accomplish in our journey. The children that have already experienced this week of fun games and lessons have emerged equipped with a foundation of knowledge they would never receive in schools and a desire for more. We were no longer just educating ourselves and being active for our children's sake, but were now directly giving them the tools to keep the light of liberty burning.

As the father of two middle-school-aged children, I have seen firsthand what our kids are learning in school these days, and it is unrecognizable. The messages that are continually reinforced into our children through television, social media, and books are not the ideas of our parents or grandparents. Clearly, we did not get here overnight nor will we be able to fix it all in our generation. Some profound changes have occurred in America, but through the sincere efforts of great people in Kentucky and around America, we can make our nation profoundly good again.

Our children are the key. They are the vessels that can carry the torch, but they are surely condemned to face tyranny if we do not fill them with principles, values, and the truth about our history. It is our responsibility to teach and instill in them who they are and all that they are capable of doing. The most important role in my life is not being the champion for KY9/12 but being a parent to my children. It is solemn personal responsibility that Lydia and I willingly accept every day. Every parent and grandparent in our group felt the same, and together we recognized the significance that Vacation Liberty School represented for our mission and our hope for the next generation. Undoubtedly, no one has ever expressed this duty better than Ronald Reagan on October 27, 1964 when he said:

"You and I have a rendezvous with destiny. We will preserve for our children this, the last best hope of man on earth, or we will sentence them to take the first step into a thousand years of darkness. If we fail, at least let our children and our children's children say of us we justified our brief moment here. We did all that could be done."

Formalization

(noun) the act of making official or legitimate by the observance of proper procedure.

AUGUST 2010

Almost a year prior, we had made a trip to D.C. on September 12th. At that point as a group, I believe, we thought we needed to fix Washington. The truth later became clear that it was not about fixing politics but about fixing ourselves and looking internally. We were thoroughly enjoying discovering for ourselves - and then educating others - about our nation's amazing history. We had transferred this learning to our children and were teaching them liberties and instilling our ideals. Reflecting on this new knowledge and basing everything on our core principles and values made it easier on each of us to do the right things in our life. Through that process, we would not only begin to restore our republic, but we would restore our honor, as well.

For months, Glenn Beck had been continually promoting the next big event to occur in Washington, D.C. In true Glenn style, even though nearly every radio show was teasing the next BIG announcement about this gathering, it was now August and the exact details were still sketchy at best. We knew these basics: there was going to be an assembly at the base of the Lincoln Memorial on August 28th, Glenn and his organization were organizing it, and we had to be there. In many ways, there were greater details about what this event would *not* be. We knew by all accounts that this was not going to be a political event or tea party. We were going to D.C., but we would not be in front of the Capitol or marching to make a statement; we would be standing between the symbolic giants of the Washington and Lincoln Memorials. We were not completely sure why yet, but we all shared the feeling that this day was going to be big, historic, and important.

The excitement had been building for months and now reached extraordinary levels. Groups of 9/12ers from across the country were coordinating busses online and planning to be there. While Glenn did his best to downplay the attendance estimates that were popping up, the reports from various state leaders was indicating that this could easily eclipse the march we had attended eleven months earlier. Kentucky alone had eleven busses prepared to make the journey compared to the two we had arranged the previous year. Though we had very little idea what the Restoring Honor Rally might have in store for us, we had inspiration to be part of it and anticipation of history being made by it.

At the same time, controversy from an opposition crowd was beginning to build as well. August 28th was the anniversary of Martin Luther King's "I Have a Dream" speech from the steps of the Lincoln Memorial. Although Glenn Beck had explained repeatedly how he had selected the date and the respect he personally felt for this great civil rights leader, it of course fell on deaf ears and accusations were being thrown from the likes of The Reverend Al. In stark contrast to the insinuations of racism or insensitivity, The 9/12 Project was about becoming the people we were the day after September 11th, when we didn't care about political parties or skin colors, but were instead united as Americans.

Still, there were now rumors of counter-protest. What exactly were they going to protest? No one outside Glenn's company even knew what the rally was completely about yet. Were they protesting the nine principles we practiced or the fact that we were open to all races, denominations, and political affiliations? I truly believe their motivation was to try to scare people and deter a large turnout, and I must be honest that they did have some impact. While we had our members mobilized and eleven busses full and ready to go, I had a personal decision that was weighing heavy on me.

As the group's leader, I knew I would be on one of those busses, but - unlike last time - my family might have the opportunity to join us on this trip. Would that be the right thing to do under these circumstances, though? I had a one-year-old baby, a twelve-year-old stepson, and a wonderful wife. What threats could this rally pose to the ones that I loved most? I was excited by the chance to once again have them by my side, but not if that meant putting them in harm's way. Ultimately, Lydia and I shared a common faith that everyone associated with this gathering would be peaceful and respectful and that it was going to be a truly historic event that our children needed to experience. In order to spare baby Sophia from the eleven-hour bus ride, Lydia and the kids would fly to Washington and be there waiting for us when we arrived. The decision was made and the family was going.

On February 12, 1809, Abraham Lincoln was born in Hardin County, Kentucky. In his death, he became one of the most admired men in history. In his life, Abraham Lincoln remained true to his Kentucky roots. We would now be making a landmark journey in the footsteps of this great president. Together, we would travel from Lincoln's birthplace of Kentucky to the steps of the Lincoln Memorial in Washington, D.C. to become part of history by joining Glenn Beck on August 28th for the Restoring Honor Rally.

To add to the excitement, our Kentucky group had also spent several months planning the second-annual national 9/12 Project reception for the evening before the rally. The first year, we organized the reception because it needed to be done and 9/12ers needed a venue to come together. The big difference in year two was our being requested by the national board to organize the reception and our working very closely with National Director Yvonne Donnelly to help coordinate the honoring of selected 9/12ers as a portion of the event.

Always happy to be of service, we jumped in with both feet and secured a venue that could hold twice the number of people as the first reception. Much like the planned August 28th rally itself, we wanted to make the reception a big and memorable event. We had grand aspirations to bring in a big name speaker, but we did not have any immediate luck securing anyone. We were not going to let that be a discouragement, though. We announced the event details, and with help from the national 9/12 Project, it went out to other groups nationwide. As anticipated, the excitement people had for the rally carried over in their enthusiasm for our reception, as well. Tickets began to sell quickly, and one month before the event, we had sold five hundred tickets.

Our event content began to take shape when we caught a lucky break courtesy of a connection within the Central Illinois 9/12 Project. We were contacted by Jon David Kahn, a fabulous musician that we were very lucky to secure to perform at the reception. We added a conservative comedian named Brad Stein as our primary entertainment for the evening and Yvonne served as the Master of Ceremonies. There was still no big name headline speaker for us to announce as that detail was yet to be finalized. Yvonne had been working on a very special guest, but even on the day of the event there were still questions if they were going to be able to attend. We simply hoped for the best and moved forward.

Our busses from Kentucky were scheduled to arrive in Washington several hours before the reception to allow us plenty of time to get prepared. Unfortunately, the enormous volume of traffic heading into the capital for the rally the following day served to delay our arrival by a few hours and raise my blood pressure quite a bit. After a mad dash from the bus, I met up with Lydia and the children who were already there waiting on us. We made the one-mile walk hurriedly with baby in tow to arrive about an hour before the announced start time of the event and we were stunned by what we saw. We walked in to find a line of well over one hundred people already waiting to get in the ballroom doors. We were simultaneously amazed, shocked, humbled, and excited. There were people in line from all around the country. We were surrounded by 9/12ers and clearly not alone anymore!

The atmosphere and spirit of the folks waiting in line quickly made us realize that everything we had been experiencing in Kentucky had been going on with others like us around the nation as well. Hundreds of 9/12ers were enthusiastically coming together for a night with their extended family. As the hour grew closer, the crowd grew larger and the end of the line had long disappeared out of our sight. It was hard to imagine that only months had passed since the time when many of us thought we were alone in our beliefs. Now as our second annual reception was ready to officially start, we were virtually overwhelmed by all the like-minded patriots looking to celebrate alongside us. When we finally opened the doors to the crowds, there were cheers of excitement.

We soon found ourselves with a room full of people and not nearly enough food or seats. This was supposed to only be a reception, and if some people had come for the food, they likely left hungry. Incidentally, they must have also missed the portion on the invitations that said light hors d'oeuvres would be served. We had hoped to encourage the assorted state groups to mingle by having tall tables with no chairs, but what resulted instead was dozens of people utilizing every available step or ledge or any other surface as a place to sit and eat.

What we did have plenty of was friendly atmosphere and an energy that permeated the room. Shortly after the doors were opened, we finally had confirmation that our special guest speaker would indeed be able to attend and was only a few minutes away from arriving. Yvonne had worked her magic and we were going to be honored to have Glenn Beck stop by our reception to receive an award and address the crowd. With the Restoring Honor Rally only hours away, Glenn's schedule was incredibly tight, which meant we needed to get the show on the road and begin the stage portion of the program immediately!

Disregarding our previously planned order of events, Yvonne took the stage and welcomed the crowd as several of us worked to clear a side entrance to the ballroom that could provide a clear passage for Glenn and his entourage. Yvonne finished her opening remarks and glanced at the door, but there was no sign of Glenn. She stalled a little longer and glanced back over, but we could only motion for her to keep talking. As she was just beginning to move ahead into the next portion of the program – and with virtually no warning - Glenn Beck was ushered like a flash through the side door and was standing on the stage beside her as the crowd went absolutely wild with excitement!

We were honored beyond words to have Glenn Beck, the very man behind the launch of The 9/12 Project as well as the next day's mammoth Restoring Honor Rally, not only stop by our reception, but to also say a few sincere words from his heart to us. We were all thankful to be there to see this man who inspired us, yet at the same time, he was there to thank us for being an inspiration to him. On behalf of The 9/12 Project members, Glenn was presented with the "Sacred Honor" award in the form of a specially-made flag symbolizing our growing movement. This was a moment that put goose bumps on every arm and tears in every eye in the room.

As memorable as that moment was, it was not the most exciting part of the evening for our Kentucky group. While working with the national board members on planning this reception, everyone agreed that we wanted to honor those 9/12ers and patriots that had exemplified the spirit of The 9/12 Project. In addition to honoring Glenn Beck during his visit, we decided to present three other special awards as a portion of the evening's program. First, the Liberty Heart Award would be awarded to a person that had made great sacrifices in the promotion of our principles. Second, the Refounders Award would go to the person that best personified those principles. Lastly, the Constitutional Champions Award would go to the person or group that best championed those principles.

It was inspiring to see Katy Abram receive the Liberty Heart. It was an honor as I was able to present Yvonne Donnelly with the Refounders Award. Words fail me, though, to describe the blend of gratitude and pride that I felt when our Kentucky 9/12 Project group was announced as the recipient of the National Constitutional Champions Award for implementing programs, educating, defending, or promoting the founding principles.

For us, that evening was a culmination of eighteen months of growth and effort by a whole state full of hard-working patriots. As members of our group stood on the stage, we were all honored and humbled to have been recognized in the company of these other amazing award recipients. Seeing Kentucky singled out from all of the 9/12 groups from around the nation due to our qualities of innovation and inspiration made us all very proud. This not only legitimized the great people of Kentucky as trendsetters, but was unshakable confirmation of where we as a group were headed.

The remainder of the reception was spent enjoying the company of our family, friends, and fellow 9/12ers. It was a blessing for me to have Lydia and the kids by my side for this year's festivities. Little Sophia even entertained us with her dance moves as Jon

David Kahn was performing one of his songs onstage. We could not have possibly asked for a better event or a better evening of inspiration to lead us into the history-making rally that awaited us the following day.

On the morning of August 28th, I headed out before Lydia and the baby and gathered with our Kentucky group about one mile away from the National Mall as we began our walk together. We were a sea of blue shirts and, of course, me with my bullhorn. We made it as far as the World War II Memorial two hours before the rally was to begin and discovered this was probably the closest we were going to make it. Thousands upon thousands of people were already there and filled the mall between us and the stage on the steps of the Lincoln Memorial which was just a speck in the distance.

For the following two hours, the crowd continued to grow and grow and grow, and it filled in every empty spot around us and far beyond. This caused me some anxiety as I had left Lydia and the kids at the hotel with plans to meet up with us just before the rally began. When we had positioned our group's little camp for the day, I chose a spot near the sidewalk to hopefully allow them to locate us easily and have access to reach us with Sophia's stroller. As the minutes passed, I watched all the possible paths to our location filled in with bodies. I became increasingly concerned as the crowd swelled that Lydia may not be able to ever find her way to us.

I should never doubt my wife's determination, though. Bless her heart, she loaded up Sophia in her baby stroller and - with twelve-year-old Aaron in tow also - made the one-mile walk into the sea of people lugging along all the necessities to keep our family comfortable for the day. We talked on our cell phones and I made my way back through the mass of humanity to meet them. Our reunited family then successfully navigated our way back to our little area with everyone else from KY9/12 slowly but surely.

By the time the rally began, I could honestly say I had never seen a crowd that size before and the numbers reported by the media will never do it justice. I will leave the exact count for historians to speculate on in the future, but even a blind squirrel could see it exceeded the 87,000 that was reported by CBS. We easily filled every available square foot around the reflecting pool, we filled the overflow area to the south, and we filled the tree lines around the perimeter all the way back to the Washington Monument.

Seconds before the rally's formal program began, reverent and stunned silence gave way to thunderous applause as a perfect V-formation of geese did their own fly-over for the crowd, in some ways as if they were a message from God of His approval on our gathering. After that surreal opener, we listened and were inspired by various speakers, musicians, and presentations. Living up to Glenn's promise, this was not a political event, and it was not a tea party. It was an event honoring great people, and it was a reflection of us. With laughter, tears, prayer, and songs, we witnessed history and took away countless memories.

Despite the heat of the August sun and the lack of personal space that the crowds created, everyone remained respectful and polite, going as far as sharing water and umbrellas with those around them. It was impossible for me to not feel calm and safe - even in this large gathering - as I stood there with little Sophia up on my shoulders and listened to the poignant and touching words being shared from the stage. Something beyond imagination was happening. Something extraordinary was taking place - something beyond mortal man's ability to fully appreciate or comprehend.

I wish I could find the words to convey the spirit that washed over the crowd during this amazing day on the National Mall. At the conclusion of the event, I sat down and tried to capture my immediate thoughts and feelings on paper in hopes of using the notes to provide e-mail and website updates to our members back in Kentucky that had been unable to make the trip with us. I also asked several of our other members to jot down their impressions of the rally. Below is a sample of the immediate reactions that we captured that weekend in the words of the people that experienced it. Hopefully, their words will help to at least begin to express the impact this event had on everyone who attended it.

"On 8/28, an estimated 750,000 to over one million people gathered in the shadow of the Lincoln Memorial to honor our heritage, honor our soldiers, and honor our heroes. Themes of faith, hope, and charity resonated throughout the Restoring Honor Rally highlighted the beginnings of the great American experiment of freedom and a faith in God that makes nations that seek Him strong. This was not a tea party, it was not a political rally, it was not about the color of our skin but it was about the content of our character, it was about Restoring Honor. This weekend we came back together to see that we are not alone; and left inspired and revived. Although this was not a march or a protest either the sounds that you may hear are the steps of a movement that will not be held back. From this weekend we have begun the next steps to Restore Honor, Restore Our Family, Restore Our Communities, and Restoring Our Republic. The media really doesn't know what to make of this weekend and to be honest it may take a few days for everything to settle in for each of us as well. There has never been an event like this before on the Mall in DC and most likely will never be another again in our lifetime. It was 2/3 church service, 2/3 military honor, 2/3 history lesson, 2/3 heroes,

and 100% inspirational. There was honesty of who we were and are and a calling for whom we should be. For those that were not there, you may never understand what this weekend was, for those of us that went we may never forget what we shared. — **Eric Wilson**

"This weekend's Restoring Honor Rally brought together hundreds of thousands of proud Americans from all walks of life. In my opinion, there was a marked contrast between this Rally and last year's 9/12 March on DC. The 2009 March on DC was an expression of frustration and anger because our shared concerns were being ignored. The roar of the crowd was like a tidal wave crashing through the streets. The 2010 Restoring Honor Rally was a gathering of faith, hope and charity - which was evident in the reverence exhibited by those in attendance. The hush of the crowd was as gentle as a baby's sigh. Ah, the difference a year can make. The future of America is in her people - not the government. We no longer await the recognition of elected officials or administrative clerks - we recognize ourselves. The best is yet to come! God Bless America." — **Anne Nagy**

"The Restoring Honor event on 8-28 was the next logical step towards returning our country to the strength of its foundation: '....that all men are created equal, that they are endowed by their Creator with certain unalienable Rights, that among these are Life, Liberty and the pursuit of Happiness.' If the firmest atheist or agnostic examined unbiased statistics of our society, the numbers would tell that America had calmer, safer and stronger communities when more of her citizens highly valued faith, honor and charity. Restoring Honor reinforced those principles and reminded me that life's "invisible" parts are its most important." — **Jim Drake**

"I will personally never forget the Restoring Honor weekend. The stories of these three days will be the worn-out stories that I tell my grandchildren decades from now. Before a single word was ever spoken from the stage, the crowd and the spirit alive within it told an amazing tale. Hundreds of thousands of everyday Americans willing to sacrifice one of the final weekends of summer to come out and stand in the hot sun to show our support for our military, our country, and our Creator. By the time the three hours of festivities were concluded, there was one central theme that spoke loudest to me and was reflected in the words of men and women on stage from a myriad of backgrounds. The message that I took to heart was that we need to realize, while we may not come to agreement on specific details of theology, the vast majority of the assorted faiths in our country share common principles that can unite us to help turn this country around." – **Justen Collins**

"It was an absolutely awesome event and this Christian Veteran Patriot would classify it as a spiritual event, not a political event. Nobody will be able to properly put it into words. You had to be there to witness the Spirit moving in the hearts of our countrymen" – **Jeff Smith** aka **Mario**

"This was a call for people to reach into their heart, and to do great things, and to stand up for a great nation." – **Lisa Williams**

While the journey to Washington and back for our group was entirely focused on the reception and rally, our trip also allowed us to receive some unique international exposure before, during, and after the event. With the build-up to the rally receiving attention in many of the mainstream media outlets, hundreds of journalists wanted to document this historic event. Even the BBC from across the pond had a curiosity and reached out to us to see if they could document our journey from a few members' perspectives. Literally hours after agreeing to participate, willing members had camera crews, boom microphones, and a production team following them around their homes, churches, and work places.

The BBC's documentary crew went as far as meeting us on the morning of our trip and joining us on the busses for the first couple legs of our journey to Washington. Now, not only did our people get up at 5am to board a crowded bus for a ten-hour trip, but they were sharing it with large cameras, production lights, and a charismatic British television host asking some off-the-wall questions. The finished product was another learning experience for our group, though. Despite our hopes that the foreign crew might be less biased than our own mainstream domestic media, the documentary painted our movement in a less-than-positive light. Several out-of-context quotes and images served to remind us how careful we needed to be with the ways in which we allowed our group to be portrayed.

On a better note - and more special to me personally - was another documentary that was being put together about the rally. I had received yet another call from one of Glenn Beck's producers. This marked the third time I had heard from them in the past year. A guy could get used to all this attention!

This time it was a representative from Mercury Radio Arts - Glenn's company which handles his radio program and many of his other multimedia productions. They were filming a documentary of the rally weekend, as well, and asked our Kentucky group to provide footage of our trip. They also asked us to conduct some video interviews during our journey using a few specific questions they provided. One of our tech-savvy members took on this project and did a marvelous job capturing the moments, energy, and essence of our trip.

When I had arrived at the rally itself, Mercury interviewed me in person and added my comments to the hours of footage they had collected. In an amazingly short time, they put together a very slickly-produced release of their 8/28 documentary. Several weeks later, when the documentary premiered on the internet, Lydia and I had a few people over at our home to watch the premiere knowing I might have a small cameo. Instead, I was shocked to see not only myself all through the video but proud at seeing others like Lisa Williams and Jeff Smith. I let a few tears slip out as they replayed - and I re-lived - the reception we hosted the evening before the rally. I was absolutely floored, though, when the final words of the documentary were mine, as I had recapped my experience into our group's video camera on the evening of 8/28.

This documentary had been put together by Glenn's production company to encapsulate that day and to bring back the emotions and feelings we had felt. It was meant to inspire us, and solidify for us the message he wanted us to take away. The Kentucky 9/12 Project was now a part of this. We were part of what had been created that weekend. We had been a part of history.

∽

SEPTEMBER 2010

We were back home from Washington and back in the pressure cooker of the Kentucky political race to Election Day. The campaign season was in full swing now, and we had one of the most-watched races in the nation right in our back yard. Tea Party darling Rand Paul was in a tight race for US Senate and there were millions of eyes on this contest. This brought the mainstream media out in full force, and the phone calls began to roll in at our house. The Washington Post, Financial Times, and CNN among many others all reached out for interviews from someone they saw as a leader of a tea party movement. It became humorous over time giving the answers repeatedly.

"We are non-partisan and we do not endorse candidates."

"I don't know. You would have to ask each person involved in the tea party movement, because I can't speak for them."

Last but not least, and my personal favorite, "that is not who we are...no comment."

The novelty of being interviewed wore off very quickly, but that was fine because they soon tired of not getting the answers they wanted. Dodging the media frenzy was actually making it much easier for us to maintain our stance of non-partisanship. Outside the media, pressure was getting equally crazy as we were being inundated every day with recommendations from campaign personnel on what we needed to be doing and complaints about what we were not already doing.

Thankfully, the spirit that still was simmering from our Washington experience set the stage for our next event. September 12th was approaching on the calendar and Justen Collins made the comment that we could not let this day go by and not at least do a little something. Everyone agreed and we decided to use the opportunity to bring people back together. We hosted a statewide picnic to serve as our "Kentucky 9/12 Appreciation Day."

In an environment filled with campaign ads everywhere you looked and candidate rallies every other day, this was a day simply for the

9/12 Project members. It was a beautiful day with great entertainment, wonderful people, and the best part: no campaign signs, no protest posters, no candidate speeches, and nothing political. People came together and rekindled that spirit and feeling we had on 8/28. This was, in essence, another huge family reunion. To me, it was kind of amazing in its own right.

We posted details about the event and said exactly what it would be and nothing more. No sales pitch. Just the facts: it was not a tea party, there would be no special guests with any name recognition, there would be no speeches, you needed to bring your own food, the musical entertainment would be someone you most likely never heard of before, so come on out and show up in the middle of nowhere on a Sunday afternoon! I guess it was somehow irresistible as a couple of hundred people showed up from miles around just to spend time with like-minded people.

KY9/12 Project Picnic

Event Details

Join other 9/12ers as we enjoy a family-friendly event to unwind and socialize with like minded patriots from around the state and find pride in our inner voice of being a 9/12er. In that spirit this will be a non-political event that will pay tribute to all of us that embody our nations founding principles. Leave your signs, pitchforks, and torches at home and bring your blanket, lawn chair, and picnic lunches and enjoy great live entertainment, share in a special award presentation to a few great patriots and groups, and more importantly have the opportunity to get to know your neighbor and meet other like minded 9/12ers from around the state.

When
Sunday, September 12, 2010 3:00pm (ET)
Where
Talon Winery   7086 Tates Creek Rd

270 KY9/12ers are going

Even the very beginning of the picnic was emotional and uplifting for me, as my daughter Sarah made her father proud by joining with Ricky Hostetler's daughters and niece to sing the national anthem. From that point, it was just a relaxed day full of good-natured people sharing their food with one another and enjoying nearly perfect weather. We had a table of group merchandise available for purchase, and were able to simply leave a fishbowl out for people to deposit their money if they choose to take anything. How honorable was this group of patriots? When the picnic ended - even with no one manning the merchandise table — there was far more money in the fishbowl than there were items purchased! That is just the kind of people that 9/12ers are.

We rounded out the picnic festivities by first handing out appreciation awards to recognize some of our hardest-working members. Next, it was time to pit our community groups against one another in a fast-paced game of Constitution trivia. Our stated goal had long been to promote education, so it was time to see how well we were doing. It turned into a very fun and spirited contest for our folks, and it was a refreshing change from our more normal activities. Watching each of the local groups building even stronger bonds by competing together as a team showed us there was even a true benefit to be found in something we had only intended to be an entertaining game. We went home from that picnic feeling even more impressed by the friends we had been blessed with through our participation in The 9/12 Project and even more proud to be 9/12ers.

∽

OCTOBER 2010

Our last couple of events had now been uplifting, inspirational, and focused on the encouraging fellowship aspect of our group's progression. With our next event, it was time to bring everyone's attention back to our drive for continuing education. We needed to extend our reach beyond learning on our own and urging our members toward lifelong pursuits of knowledge. We had a desire to begin reaching out to other groups and people not in our fold to enlighten them as well. This desire led us to help host a large-scale event we called the Freedom Liberty Conference.

The concept for the conference was a day-and-a-half-long education forum with over thirty hours of training, featured speakers, and a strong focus on heritage-based education, faith, values, and tools people could take home and begin to use on their own. For this conference, we teamed up with the Northern Kentucky Tea Party and the Heartland Tea Party, and everyone's efforts and contributions were invaluable to this event's success.

I will admit that bringing different movements with different strategic goals together to plan and implement a single event had many, many challenges. I would be dishonest if I didn't say there were days where I didn't think the conference would happen and other days that I just wanted to walk away from the entire project. We struggled through it, though, and learned as we went along. Thankfully, the ultimate product was an absolutely huge success by every measure.

The conference was held exactly one month prior to an historic election, and as I mentioned earlier, we had one of the most-watched Senate races going on in Kentucky. There was intense pressure to couple this conference with a political rally and provide tables and forums for candidates, but that was not what this event was about. This event was about laying foundations and enlightening people.

We had some of the country's top recognized trainers from American Majority, FreedomWorks, and the National Center for Constitutional Studies. We had break-out sessions on the faith of our Founding Fathers, the Declaration of Independence, Saul Alinsky's "Rules for Radicals," and Developing America's Great Success Formula. Everything we planned was designed to lay the ground work and provide the tools people needed for self-education and action.

In spite of the challenges of putting this conference together, in spite of the personalities that sometimes clashed, in spite of the minor glitches before and even during the conference, the people who paid to attend had a wonderful time. As always, we fretted over each mishap behind the scenes, but just like every other event we had held, the people that came didn't see or know any of them. What they saw and experienced was an education conference that exceeded their expectations. The comment cards we had distributed to attendees all came back with great reviews about all aspects of the event.

Like most of things we had done recently, we went big with this conference. This was easily one of the largest events in terms of planning time, dollars spent, logistics required, and scheduled duration. It also turned out as one of the most successful. Not because of the surveys saying everyone had a good time, though that was encouraging. Not because we added new members, as at this point we were no longer measuring our success on the number of people on our distribution list. Not because we actually turned a modest profit, which was a definite first for our events. This conference was a success because it accomplished our primary strategy of education. We had pulled all of this off while never deviating from our primary values and principles, but by promoting them instead. The Freedom Liberty Conference, like the 8/28 rally, our September picnic, and the local meetings, was an example of what was possible when we remained true to our mission and focused on who we were and where we were going.

∽

NOVEMBER 2010

We may not have been endorsing candidates as a group, but we were not oblivious to the elections going on, and we truly understood the importance they held. We encouraged our members to be active in whatever way they saw fit for themselves. Some would go out to support candidates, going door to door, and making phone calls. Hopefully, all the members would exercise their personal responsibility to cast their votes, as well. We just drew the line at deciding that it was up to us to tell our members who to support. We were not looking to become an extension of any political party.

Without doubt, the election's significance was not lost on our members. Many of them worked on campaigns to support their own respective candidates, just not as official representatives of The 9/12 Project. We even had a few members who ran for local offices and some won their elections!

There were many of us that wanted to share this evening together and enjoy it in a 9/12 way. We met informally - without wearing large campaign buttons and without the party insiders present - to watch the results. I don't know how to explain this, but it was "politics without the politicking." About fifty 9/12ers met at a local sports bar and enjoyed each other's company just as much as we enjoyed the results. Included in our numbers was the newly-elected constable for the district who is himself a dedicated 9/12 member.

We shared more than the excitement of the results. We shared the bond of a common perspective on what the night's results meant. No one had seen these types of results in over seventy years, and it did send a message. It was a message that could no longer be ignored. The liberty movement had made a statement and was elevated to another level of credibility and influence.

What we also saw was the power of people waking up and voting, and we knew that they would not go back to sleep. I don't care what others may say, emotions do wear off, and apathy can return. But a truly informed voter will never go away.

We also awoke to see the day after the election. With the fervor of campaigning now over, the importance of who we were and what we needed to do became even more important. We were never about re-electing a party, but re-educating a public and that responsibility was not any closer to being accomplished now than it was the day before the election. Our mission had not changed at all, and we, the grassroots people making up the Kentucky 9/12 Project were not going away any time soon.

NOVEMBER 13, 2010

I am not ashamed to say that my wife and I remain the quintessential average Americans. We are proud of who we are and what we are doing. We are guided by a set of principles and promote a standard of values. We see what is happening in this great nation and passionately desire to restore the republic that we love. We are giving up sitting idly by in apathy in exchange for a glimmer of hope for our children's future. My wife and I are loving spouses to each other and concerned parents for our children. Many of the days or evenings we once spent at home are now spent working to bring about fundamental change in people's minds and this nation's direction.

Exactly twenty months have passed since we first ventured out to find out we were not alone. My initial ambition of finding like-minded people has been overwhelmingly realized. Our early milestones of just keeping a fledgling group together and getting everyone to and from Washington, D.C. safely have now come and gone twice. All of these goals met have served to bring about the realization that our mission has just really begun.

There is a greater focus now than ever within the group, as well as a strategic vision of what we want to accomplish. Not surprisingly, it revolves around the same things that started this movement twenty months earlier. It is a common idea based on principles and values, an understanding of the importance of education and an informed electorate, an empowerment to act on your own, and a support group and network of like-minded patriots.

As much as things remain the same, this is a new day for the movement and we are no longer a disjointed collective searching for direction. We are organized now and carry a renewed sense of enduring purpose. We have been legitimized through media coverage and public perception; earning respect from some while becoming a target for others. Finally – and for the first time in our journey - we have resources and money as well as the brand new concerns and responsibilities that come with them.

It has become obvious now that "business as usual" will require more of a true "business approach." Several observations combine to encourage us to take the next step in the evolution of our group. We realize continuing to fulfill our mission will require additional centralized planning and additional resources. We can look just a few short years down the road and anticipate the need for a more formal organization to sustain our movement.

Our decision at this point was clear, and a meeting was called to carry out the final act of making things official. We determined that organizing as a social welfare organization under section 501(c)(4) of the Internal Revenue Code would best fit our new organization. While our purchases may not be tax-exempt and donations made to us may not be tax-deductible, it is still a not-for-profit status that carries a lot less regulations making it perfect for social movements like ours. If people are going to donate to us, it will not be out of desire for a deduction but because they believe in our mission and want to help in what we are doing. We remain non-partisan and a-political under this status, but we can still advocate for issues that our group deems appropriate.

By signing official articles of incorporation, we were taking away some of the flexibility and "flying by the seat of our pants" and replacing them with formal meetings and regularly-required filings. As board members, we had always felt a solemn responsibility for what we were doing, but now we would also have defined accountability. On the other side, though, we would limit our liabilities and create a new umbrella organization that was capable of bigger and better things. We would have new freedoms to raise needed funds instead of going from event-to-event just trying to cover our costs.

The purpose and spirit of the people involved has not changed, and they have been and will continue to be the driving force. This remains a truly grassroots movement rooted in nine principles and twelve values focused on rediscovering who we are and teaching others the heritage of what makes this nation great. The formalization at the top has evolved out of necessity and - with or without a signature on a paper - there is now an organization and defined collective focus on a unified objective.

We were not changing to a top-down organization as KY9/12 would always exist to support the bottom-up grassroots needs. Little, if anything, can ever be accomplished until individuals embrace their personal responsibility to heed that undeniable call to action within themselves. Once they choose to engage, it is about people coming together and sharing a set of values and vision. It is about spreading that unity to neighborhoods and communities and around our state. It is about groups with different people and different paths embracing common objectives.

Our goal is to create a structure that combines the best of both worlds. We would encourage personal responsibility and an organic grassroots nature to allow for the freedom needed to grow and develop. We would also provide the protection and organization that could help development and provide focus. We would not control or dictate to the local groups, but would maintain a subservient role to them. We had seen that with the right arrangement an idea could come from an individual in Owensboro, be expanded upon by others in Lexington, be communicated through a network to everyone in Kentucky, and then be circulated nationwide to 9/12 groups in every state.

Anxious to make our new structure a reality, twelve of our members gathered in our home on a Saturday afternoon in the middle of November. The faces that came through the door were more than

just familiar now; they were sincere friends that all shared the same
views. Many of us had been there when this whole thing started and
contributed differently along the way. Scattered around our living room
with Lydia and I were the people that represented the backbone of the
Kentucky 9/12 Project:

There were Jim and Niki Drake who we first met on that March
13th and had since been my close confidants and right-hand people.

There was Anne Nagy who coordinated monthly meetings with all
the local leaders of 9/12 groups from around our state.

There was Justen Collins who first became a friend at work then
became the genesis for our group's social media exposure.

There was Lisa Williams that actually first corresponded with us
even before the kick-off event and had helped at every activity since.

There were Lisa and Jeff Abler who were there for our kick-off,
continued to be active, and helped organize a national phenomenon in VLS.

There were Jim and Rita Ramsay who helped in organizing local
groups and served as the educational authority for our group.

There was Suzanne Meyer who had been involved from early on
and handled meeting communications and schedule coordination for
the group.

Most importantly – while not physically present – there in spirit with
us were the thousands of loyal and dedicated 9/12ers across Kentucky
whose tireless work and motivation had kept our group going strong
for the past twenty months.

Together, we had come such a long way. We had witnessed and played
a part in the ups and downs and the occasional stumbles of the group.
We had overcome times when we each felt isolated and frustrated
while looking for something or someone to bring us together. Each of
us had contributed to a renewed determination that our group could

make a difference and find a collective identity. We had all participated in trying to help find that new identity and sorting through the chaos from activity-to-activity to help define a movement. As a group, we had finally graduated from unfocused random events to a new era of organizational discipline. To complete the transition, twelve of us would put pen to paper and take this next partially-symbolic step of formal incorporation.

Twenty months had passed and now another meeting was to set to begin. This new assembly was slightly different and would be formally called to order. After a few other formalities, the preamble to our new constitution and by-laws would be presented:

> *Through Divine Providence, We as citizens of the Commonwealth of Kentucky and the United States of America, do come together in order to protect and preserve our Representative Republic, re-establish and promote the proven Principles, and ensure continuing Liberty for Ourselves and our Posterity, do formally institute the Kentucky 9/12 Project and establish this Constitution.*

On March 13, 2009, approximately 140 people gathered in a pizza place looking for a chance to meet like-minded people and unexpectedly became part of a new social movement – The 9/12 Project.

On November 13, 2010, exactly 12 people gathered in our home hoping to take their movement to another level and confidently started a new social organization – The Kentucky 9/12 Project, Inc.

A Call to Action

"How strangely will the Tools of a Tyrant pervert the plain Meaning of Words!"
-- Samuel Adams

This book was never intended to be about me nor did I really set out to write about the Kentucky 9/12 Project. This book was in many ways meant to be about you. I know many may read this and see similarities in our stories and our struggles or share similar journeys or ideas. I hoped you might find a connection with our chronicles, a reassurance that you are not alone, and a roadmap you could share with others.

If you are still seeking the motivation and inspiration to begin your own journey, hopefully this book can provide them. If you retain nothing else, remember that the key is personal responsibility – the first steps are up to you. Nothing that I have personally done is unique to me or special enough to deserve an entire book's focus on me. I simply did the one thing that millions of others have finally done in recent years: *SOMETHING!*

All liberty needs to survive is for ordinary people to rise up and become active. May our stories empower you and help lead you from isolation and irritation to determination and hope. I challenge each of you to take the following actions in your life, beginning right now:

Begin at your dinner table. I suggest that you start with yourself and the people in your own home. Educate yourself and discover who you are. Talk to your family about your Values and Principles. Ground yourself and your family first and foremost in these principles and talk about what is going on in our country and what it means to your family.

Reach out to your neighbors, family, and friends. When you enlighten others, you will find that you are not alone. Communication with your neighbors is vital to the process of protecting our country. Hold or attend weekly or monthly meetings in your neighborhood or town. Gather in living rooms, coffee houses or restaurants. Share your thoughts and ideas.

Be a part of something. At some point in life, standing up for what is right has to take precedence over the alternative of doing nothing. I would encourage you to be part of The 9/12 Project and join us or a group in your area. Even if you do not join this movement, find an organization that you can join and support. There are many great groups out there fighting the fight and spreading the message of liberty. Be part of something and find one or more of these groups that fit your objectives, goals, and values. Don't just join, but try to get involved. Contact them and ask what you can do, go to meetings, and keep in touch with what they are working on.

Every single generation is seemingly faced with a crossroads that may determine the future for generations to come. This is the critical point of directional change for a country that has caused empires to fall or a fledgling nation to prosper beyond belief. I do not believe it is an exaggeration to say that we may be at that crossroads and together we may be the key. You have a choice. You can be the person you were on September 10, 2001 - ignorant to imminent danger, your head in the sand, and possibly in apathy. Or you can be that person you were on September 12th, rising to action and united with your fellow Americans. On that day, we stood shoulder-to-shoulder, unconcerned about our different religious beliefs, skin colors, or political parties. We were united to protect the greatest country in the world.

I know it can be intimidating when it seems like you are a lone voice, and it appears you are surrounded by your adversaries. Trust me when I say, reality is much different. The truth is we are the natural governing majority and the masses, if communicated to, believe as you do. We have not moved; the government has. The answer for what is wrong is not policy or politics but principles. Consider with me the following and be honest if this is what you believe as well:

America is good. We believe America is a good place. Though we may have lost our way over the years, we have good people and a solid foundation, if we only build on both of them. I am sorry, but just look at America. Look what people can achieve when left unrestricted by the bonds of government regulations. Look at the spirit that founded this country and the documents they provided to guide us today. We may have strayed from much of that, but the elements still exist and the best days can still be ahead of us. We believe America is a good place.

I believe in God and He is the center of my life. By the grace of God and through His faith, we believe that all things work together for good, to them that love God, to them that are the called according to His purpose. Through grace we not only believe in God and He is the center of our life, but we believe that we did not place Him there but He was and shall always be there, because He is sovereign.

I must always try to be a more honest person than I was yesterday. We believe that is our responsibility. Trust me when I say that sometimes I fail at this one and make mistakes, but everyday I am provided a clean slate to try again. We will make it our mission to be better tomorrow than we are today.

My spouse and I are the ultimate authority, not the government. We believe family is important and sacred. It is not hard to be a mom or dad, but it takes a monumental responsibility to take on being a parent. We will be the influences for our children and assume the accountability for our family. We will instill the values, work ethic, and duty that they will replicate to their children and their children's children.

If you break the law, you pay the penalty. Justice is blind, and no one is above it. There is right and wrong, and there should be no politics in justice. We are responsible citizens, and we trust that if we break a law, there is a consequence. We know and should be accountable for our own actions and believe that others should accept that responsibility and be held accountable for theirs.

I have a right to life, liberty and the pursuit of happiness, but there is no guarantee of equal results. This phrase may be part and parcel of everything the Founding Fathers believed and meant for us - "Life, Liberty, and the Pursuit of Happiness." By Divine Providence, we are given these inalienable rights and government can never become a god and regulate, take away, or ensure their outcome.

I work hard for what I have, and I will share it with who I want. The government cannot force me to be charitable. You cannot redistribute social equality. Forced redistribution of wealth with hostility toward individual property rights, under the guise of charity and/or justice should never be the consequence of hard work and success.

It is not un-American for me to disagree with authority or to share my personal opinion. We are not radicals, racists, or extremists that want this country to fail. We want socialism and progressivism to not succeed, and it is not anti-American to stand for the founding principles and speak out against an attack on liberty. We believe it is not un-American to peacefully assemble at the reflecting pool in Washington, D.C. with absolutely no violent acts requiring police intervention, no destruction of any property, cleaning up after ourselves, and providing a message of character.

Finally, **we believe that government works for us. I do not answer to them, they answer to me.** They are employed by us and answer to us, we do not answer to them. We have finally cracked that coded message in the preamble to the Constitution of The United States of America. Looking closely, the first three words are like 36-point font. "We the People" know that our rights don't come from the government, but we give a fiduciary responsibility to them in which they are failing. We believe we are given the duty to hold those people accountable and continuously purge them from offices through the ballot box to ensure and restore our republic.

Just think of the previous nine things I have mentioned and pause to consider this: do you agree with at least seven of those nine principles? If so, you are in the company of over one million other proud Americans and can call yourself a 9/12er! Please take a moment and go to www.the912project.com and find a group that you can become involved with locally.

Today is just the beginning; you are part of something much larger. Understand you are not alone, and we need to work together. As an individual, our power may be limited, but when we bond together it is limitless.

Remember you are not alone and that WE SURROUND THEM!

Acknowledgements

The famous declaration of George Washington is applicable for us now, as "the hand of Providence has been so conspicuous in all this" that we must first thank God for the unlikely convergence of paths He orchestrated to bring us together as friends and collaborators on this undertaking. We also want to express our thanks and great respect to Glenn Beck for launching The 9/12 Project and daily inspiring us to question all things with boldness in pursuit of the truth. Our profound appreciation and admiration go out to all the KY9/12ers who made this book possible by faithfully walking with us through this journey and supporting all the efforts with their enthusiastic attendance and generous donations. We are also grateful to the spirited 9/12 groups all across America that are embodying our Principles and Values in their lives and communities each day. Lastly, we express our sincere thanks to Yvonne Donnelly for her assistance with this endeavor as well as her tireless work to advance our movement in her role as National Director of The 9/12 Project.

Eric - I thank and dedicate this book to the one that makes me whole and is the love of my life, my wife Lydia; who gave me the inspiration to become active and the perspective to stay vigilant. My hope is this may be one more piece to provide for our children - Sophia, Sarah, and Aaron – so that we may pass the torch of liberty and principles on to them. For the many others that personally touched our lives and influenced every aspect of this journey, thank you. I could endlessly write each of your names, but my hesitation is not the ones to add but any possibility of the one I would unintentionally neglect. Each of you have become dear friends and invaluable to me and the liberty movement, and I hope you see yourselves and your influences within these pages. Finally, I want to thank the initial 140 people that came out on March 13, 2009 to a small family pizza place in Lexington, Kentucky, and who showed me that I was not alone and gave us the strength to become active.

Justen - I first have to thank the three great loves of my life. I thank my amazing wife and head cheerleader, Samantha, for her unconditional love and ability to handle my routine insanity with such grace. I thank my eldest son, Oz, for sacrificing countless hours of playtime with dad to make this book possible. I thank my new son, Stu, whose impending birth was the deadline I was striving to beat with the completion of this work, though he foiled my plans by unexpectedly showing up eighteen days early. I must also thank Tony and Janey Collins for being far greater parents than I ever deserved. I am honored to call Jeff "Mario" Smith a friend, and his story and spirit have done more to inspire me than he could ever know. There are so many others that I will not have space here to thank, but I must mention that my life would be far less fulfilling without: Eric, Dakota, and Trooper Collins, Jean and Jerry Jones, Charlie, Meagan, and Carly Henline, Jonathan Buhl, Ken Prevette, and a little guy named Wolf Rabern who will one day be a featured character in my first fiction novel. Lastly, I dedicate this book to the memory of Ed Cline whose death when I was fifteen years old changed my life. While I lost the best friend I will ever have, I gained the motivation to live every day in a way that will make him proud as he watches from above.

Appendix:

On the Origin of Social Movements

Abstract:

Being in the business of looking for causal relationships and trying to recreate patterns, I set out to better understand social movements and what ingredients it would take to recreate one, and more importantly, make one successful and keep it going. I quickly became confused; looking at other groups that were within our movement, I saw different paths and ideologies. I then studied other movements, such as the Promise Keepers, the Protestant Reformation, the Methodist Church in England, the Civil Rights Movement, the Socialist Movement, and even Alcoholics Anonymous. While I could distinguish similarities, I began to see parts of each movement that did not fit a clean blueprint for that movement itself. Reading academia, it was soon clear that they did not have the answers either. I read nine different theories that might suit one example but were problematic for many others. This was clearly not a one-size-fits-all situation and nothing seemed to fit a small box.

The answer came to me by beginning to look at social movements organically. While a movement may have a single point of origin, as it breeds new members and develops other smaller reference groups, some become isolated and develop new paths. In addition, each faction could have multiple influences that determine how the group reacts and what it may do. From here, pieces began to fit together a little bit better. I could begin to see theories as elements to a larger whole and explanations to movements' evolution. I could now understand with much more clarity why within one movement you may have protest, educational outreach, be formalized in one geographic area while unrest and chaos still persist in another. This concept was the genesis of this section and it is from this perspective that I offer my opinions on the Origin of a Social Movement. My sincere hopes are that you may glean insight or it will spur thought, so that you may sustain or continue the development of a meaningful social cause.

∽

What is a social movement?:

"Our power may be limited as individuals, but it's limitless when we bond together." - Glenn Beck

Much of what cannot be accomplished on your own can be done in groups of people who share common goals. A decentralized group of individuals coming together to sustain a campaign in support a social goal is a powerful force that can change the landscape of policy and majority thought. This is the intuitive purpose of a social movement, and in that, it is not difficult to understand why they are formed and how they become influential. Defining what elements make up a successful or unsuccessful movement or sequence of events to recreate or sustain one is much more difficult.

In many ways, it is easier to say everything that a social movement is not exactly. A movement cannot be a person, but must be constituted by a collective. It is always bigger than any individual and needs group-think and actions to be impactful. A movement is not merely a crowd, because a crowd is unable to maintain any organization and motivation capable of sustaining membership through periods of inactivity. A crowd is not capable of the planning and coalescence necessary to sustain a campaign, and you must have individuals and leaders. It must be a good balance between organization and chaos. Even then, when you may have the perfect balance of leaders and leaderless, individuality and reference group, and enterprise and anarchy, you still are dependant on networks, resources, opposition, and other catalysts out of your control.

In some ways, the birth of a new movement may be more similar to the origins of life. For any movement to materialize and prosper, it must have the right combination of elements, people, timing, and other factors working in concert. With all these elements working together in different ways and different times, no two movements evolve exactly alike and instead adapt to their unique environment and cause. What make each movement unique are the organic nature, and this spontaneous uprising and grassroots materialization of them, and the individual factors that influence and impact its development.

Considering this, we need to give up the ideas of putting the pieces together like we are building something inanimate, but look at this as giving birth to a new life. Additionally, the concept of a social movement as stages of some kind of coherent structure may be troublesome, but instead we may look at it as a distribution of junctures across a population. Typically, a movement is viewed as a single long wave or normal distribution curve to help explain the beginning and end of cycles and visualize the growth of the movement in stages. I believe this may be misleading or even inherently wrong, and instead, there are usually multiple smaller waves within larger waves or strands that change and adapt separately over time. The transition perhaps may be compared best to that in the study of adaptive evolution. Similar to the way a species maintains a common trait, it will still evolve when the distribution of characteristics within a breeding population changes in adaptation to its environment. Although some may be able to paint, with a large brush, stages of development that most social movements tend to experience; a deeper look will uncover various strands, co-evolution or even co-operation, genetic drift, and waves within waves.

Types of social movements: There is no single, standard typology of social movements. As various scholars focus on different aspects of movements, different schemes of classification emerge. Hence, any social movement may be described in terms of several dimensions. (Adapted impart by Aberle, 1966 and Blumer, 1969) These may be the more common and are focused more on the objective and views of the movement versus the make up or tactics.

	Idealistic	Action	
Magnitude of change	Reform – Wants to preserve or return to the existing values and / or stop social change from going foreword.	Reactionary – Opposition to change and avocation of a restoration of a previous state of social affairs.	Conservative
	Progressive – Argues for new social arrangement and seeks to change the collective usually within societal means.	Revolutionary – Advocates replacement of existing values by overthrowing old social order and creating a new one.	Foreword-thinking

Rate of change

On the right to left axis (figure 1) is the rate of change or the movement's objectives both strategic and tactical. The far left represents the most idealistic views and generally leads to a certain level of utopian thought. Their focus is not necessarily what is currently happening but promotion of change for future states. Usually, the strategic objectives are not to change a policy or be a counter movement but are slower in their influence. More often, their objectives are to convert majority thought and institute new or renewed social order. This is accomplished through education, propaganda, and becoming part of the fabric of community acceptance. To the far right of the chart is the opposite and is very reactionary to current events and opposition. They desire more rapid precipitous change and their objectives is an immediate modification of policy or replacing entire existing structures. They are much more action-oriented and less concerned about majority opinion and accomplish their objectives through protest and potential civil disobedience or actions to draw attention to its movement.

Going up and down or top to bottom on the axis of the chart (figure 1) will provide you the magnitude or direction of change and provides some course to the movement's views. In many ways, you may look at this axis as the middle is current views in time or status quo and going down is new revolutionary thought and going up is more traditional or time-honored beliefs. At the top are generally the beliefs that we have gone away from traditional thought and the need to return policy or values to a previous view. At the bottom is the opposite once again in the thought that the previous or current views need to be replaced with new thoughts and ideas.

Reform - Wants to preserve or return to the existing values and / or stop social change by institutional means. (Most interest groups and value-oriented groups. Also includes some think tanks. Many evangelistic groups are good examples including the Promise Keepers. Another perfect example of a movement that fits this quadrant is The 9/12 Project, in that it is a value-based movement that desires a return to the proven principles America was founded on and attempts to accomplish this through education and outreach of instruction.)

Revolutionary – Advocates replacement of existing values by overthrowing old social order and creating a new one. (Consist mainly of advocates of change and may include some underground movements and more radical elements of other social movements. Examples of various Revolutionary movements are the Protestant Reformation movement or more timely specialized human rights movements such as Civil Rights movement or Women's Liberation. All of these desire to reorganize society in accordance to their own ideological beliefs.)

Reactionary - Opposition to change and avocation of a restoration of a previous state of social affairs. (Can include counter movements or activist groups such as Anti-gun or Pro-Life movements. The modern day Tea Party movement would fit here and while fiscally and limited government-focused for the most part, they are reactionary to current policies as they occur. More overarching through protest and actions, they are attempting to stop the progression of new social orders and revert to previous proven policies and values.)

Progressive - Argues for new social arrangement and seeks to change the collective, usually within societal means. (This may include groups with specific beliefs in a future state or other utopian movements. Socialist or Progressive movement, Green movement, and some spiritual groups such as Hare Krishna, or even some more modern religious groups fit this quadrant well and try to establish themselves as the expectable norm through a collectiveness culture and avant-garde attitude.)

Common elements or traits of a social movement: As a collective, a social movement is characterized by the emergent or coalesces around common elements, social structure, and its culture. Much like the traits in species, no matter what life cycle or strand, common structural and cultural elements can be defined and are unique to the overall movement. These are the more universal elements that must exist and may define the movement.

Collective identity - This would be the group's self-image shaped by, but in turn shaping, the consciousness of individual participants. It may also be imagined as a kind of template or filter that the group and members use to process new information and shift the movement forward. This identity is generally based on previously widely-held beliefs of the participants and becomes the implied definition or beliefs of the group as a whole.

Movement cultures - The shared values, styles, behaviors, language, and / or traditions forms a group definition by which a social movement marks itself as unique. The movement's ideology may be the most important and visible culture, but there is usually many unspoken that help connect individuals to the movement and assist in the branding of the culture. These unspoken cultures may also include common language, symbols or icons, clothing, colors, location, anniversary of an event, etc.

Strategic objectives - Broadly defined, this is the target or end goal of a movement that must be achieved to make its strategies and actions successful. Although this is rarely clearly stated, it may become easily identifiable and intuitive to its membership. This is generally dictated in many ways by the origin type and will define the evolution of the movement.

Relative deprivation - People are moved to action as a result, not from absolute changes in their conditions, but of changes relative to their perception of those with whom they compare themselves. Although this has been used to explain the start of a social movement, it may better define an element of the gap, whether real or perceived, between where the collective or individuals are and where they believe they should or are entitled to be. It usually includes a reinterpretation of history, a vision of the utopia that the success of the movement will achieve, and a projection of the disastrous consequences if they fail or the opposition wins.

Collective enterprise - While this term has been used to define a "social movement" as an element, we are referring to the characteristics by which members work together as a group under a system of collectivism. We have stated that a successful movement is both organization and chaos, and this is the unique balance of structure and spontaneity; combining centralized features with decentralized ones. This proves, perhaps, that no organization can be truly leaderless. Nevertheless, these features of leaderless organizations explain in part the organic nature and life of mass movements. This element, although more difficult to explain, is important as the way the movement is formed and determinant growth.

Organic elements of a social movement: There are many elements that constitute a social movement, but within the collective enterprise there are four primary characteristics that evolve as the movement evolves. These elements are adaptive then in nature and more likely determine the activities of the movement.

Individuals - A movement will not begin or be sustained without the actions first of an individual decision. These individuals acting on behalf of the collective change depending on the demographics and life cycle of the movement. People are both rational and emotional and act accordingly. In the early stages, the followers typically are deeply committed with an almost fanatical dedication to the movement's values. As the movement progresses, the participants generally are more informed and less deeply committed and may even develop reservations.

Membership or reference group - The exact size of a movement is almost impossible to determine for membership is usually not formal, which places a premium on faith and loyalty to the collective identity. The collective and groups of individuals most often become reference groups that provide individuals confirmation of their beliefs and new and deviant view of social reality. As membership grows, it obviously becomes more diverse and broad, bringing new elements and characteristics in to the movement. It is these smaller groups that form that may determine different strands and independent groups have the capability to evolve separately at different rates.

Champion or leaders - A social movement does not possess legitimate leaders in the sense of being endowed with authority through some formal process. Leaders must constantly substantiate their claims to leadership by demonstrating the effectiveness of their influence on the followers. These champions bring unique personalities, resources, and attributes that help define directionally the movement's evolution and focus. Most frequently as the movement progresses or evolves the agents of that change will evolve as well precipitating that change. These are some of the primary champions we have chosen to define:

Charismatic - leader with obvious charisma and communication skills that symbolizes the collective identity and movement culture. Generally, the influence at the earliest stages and inception but rarely maintains an active role through the entire movement evolution.

Thinker – a more rational leader that appeals more to individual's intellect. For most reform or progressive movements, intellectuals usually play some sort of leadership role at some point contributing to the development of ideology of the movement.

Agitator – the leader that reacts and is generally personally led by more emotion and appeals to individual's fear or frustrations. These are most frequently present in revolutionary and reactionary movements and propagate continual incendiary actions.

Supporter – a more localized figure with influence or perceived power that reflects and promotes the collective identity. These are the most common as leaders of isolated or smaller networks within the group.

Administrator – leader who is more concerned with the practical matters of the movement or strategic objectives and usually possesses good organizational and leadership skills. As movements endure and focus on longer-term objectives or develop tangible resources over time, these leaders will arise.

Actions or events - We use the term in a more general sense to encompass different types of actions by the movement. It may range from staging protest or marches to waging a specific action in opposition or in favor of a belief. It just as easily may be writing influential articles or books or training and educational outreach. Some movements utilize interpersonal relations to enhance unity and encourage small more-isolated networks or groups so members can meet informally. These institute a type of event in itself allowing for members to actually feel less isolated from the movement as scattered participants. Overall, any action or event may be used in part to serve the participants to ensure them of the size, strength, and potential success of the movement and to reinforce the relative deprivation of the participants. Early on, these may be larger, generalized, and unfocused, but over time become more refined and structured campaigns. The number of actions will either diminish or accelerate in time depending on the movement and can drastically alter the evolution of a movement.

Environmental or external elements that impact a social movement: Adaptation may cause a gain of new direction or actions for a movement or the loss of unneeded or non-value added actions.

These adaptations are generally as a cause, in support of, or in response to elements outside of the internal control of the movement and defined by external factors.

Opposition - The primary source of conflict and is perceived as the obstacle to the strategic objective of the movement. They, in themselves, may act as a catalyst and continuously feed the movement with an unstable state of disharmony between incompatible beliefs and provide an external target for discontent and actions. It is important to note that this could be an overall drift of society and not an individual group of people or policy.

Network and communications - These are the social ties linking individuals and localized smaller groups and centralized elements of the movement. This acts as the infrastructure and these may take the form of large rallies where information is disseminated to mass crowds, smaller local groups, or isolated links to tie individuals directly to centralized controlled networks. The speed and accuracy at which information may be disseminated may determine the direction and rate of change for a movement.

Resources - Resources may be viewed as properties of a group and as resources that may be transferred to others. They may include: knowledge, money, media, labor, solidarity, legitimacy, and external support. These may obviously shape, dictate, or hinder the actions of a movement depending on what resources are available and what the group does with these resources. Likewise, cooperation can occur in between the evolution of two different movements to share resources or a movement may even evolve as a resource for another movement.

Opportunities - These may range in part from political, educational, or societal and provide potential catalyst for actions. Any of these may be triggers, events, and reasons relative to the reactants that modifies or increases the rate of evolution of the movement. Also, opportunities which are missed or misinterpreted may play a determining factor in the growth or the ultimate failure of a movement.

Life cycles of a social movement: It is clear that sustained social movements do undergo significant changes during its existence. While we argue that invariant stages or a linear approach fail to support the evolution or organic nature of a movement, we will look at four very broad cycles of most movements' progression. Even though we will review these cycles, it should be noted that a movement may have multiple different strands that can coexist and be at different cycles concurrently. Movements may also move in and out of various cycles in different orders or even repeat cycles if conditions allow for it. Most importantly, the characteristics, sequence, length of time, and magnitude of each cycle may vary greatly from movement to movement.

Progression of Social Movements

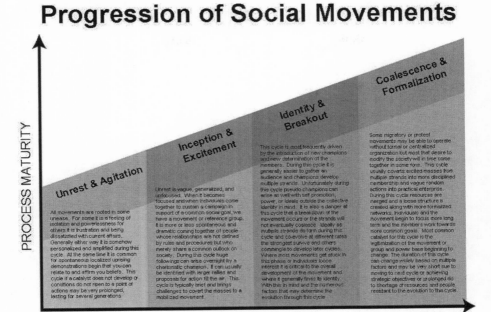

PROCESS MATURITY

Coalescence & Formalization

Identity & Breakout

Inception & Excitement

Unrest & Agitation

All movements are rooted in some unease. For some it is a feeling of isolation and powerlessness for others it is frustration and being dissatisfied with current affairs. Generally either way it is somehow personalized and amplified during this cycle. At the same time it is common for spontaneous localized uprising demonstrations begin that you can relate to and affirm you beliefs. This cycle if a catalyst does not develop or conditions do not ripen to a point of actions may be very prolonged, lasting for several generations.

Unrest is vague, generalized, and unfocused. When it becomes focused and when individuals come together to sustain a campaign in support of a common social goal, we have a movement or reference group. It is more or less spontaneous and dramatic coming together of people whose relationships are not defined by rules and procedures but who merely share a common outlook on society. During this cycle huge followings can arise overnight by a charismatic champion. It can usually be identified with large rallies and proposals for action fill the air. This cycle is typically brief and brings challenges to covert the masses to a mobilized movement

This cycle is most frequently driven by the introduction of new champions and new determination of the members. During this cycle it is generally easier to gather an audience and champions develop multiple strands. Unfortunately during this cycle pseudo champions can arise as well with self promotion, power, or ideals outside the collective identity in mind. It is also a danger at this cycle that a break down of the movement occurs or the strands will not eventually coalesce. Ideally as multiple strands do form during this cycle and co-evolve at different rates the strongest survive and others commingle to develop later cycles. Where most movements get stuck in this phase or individuals loose interest it is critical to the overall development of the movement and where it generally finds its identity. With this in mind and the numerous factors that may determine the evolution through this cycle

Some migratory or protest movements may be able to operate without formal or centralized organization but most that desire to modify the society will in time come together in some form. This cycle usually coverts excited masses from multiple strands into more disciplined membership and vague random actions into practical enterprise. During this cycle resources are merged and a loose structure is created along with more formalized networks. Individuals and the movement begin to focus more long term and the members work towards more common goals. Most common catalyst for this cycle is the legitimization of the movement or group and power base beginning to change. The duration of this cycle can change widely based on multiple factors and may be very short due to moving to next cycle or achieving strategic objectives or prolonged do to shortage of resources and people resistant to the evolution to this cycle.

Time & Evolution

Unrest / Agitation - All movements are rooted in some unease. For some, it is a feeling of isolation and powerlessness, for others, it is frustration and being dissatisfied with current affairs. Generally either way, it is somehow personalized and amplified during this cycle. At the same time, it is common for spontaneous localized demonstrations to begin that a person can relate to and that affirm an individual's beliefs. This cycle, if a catalyst does not develop or conditions do not ripen to a point of actions, may be very prolonged, lasting for several months, years, or even generations.

Focus -   Uprising of Charismatic Champion(s)
               Create networks
               Generate public awareness
               Personalize the problem focus on beliefs

Hazards -   Pushing people into next cycle before they are ready
             Feeling overwhelmingly powerless
             Not recognizing or understanding the underline building
             conditions

Inception / Excitement - Unrest is vague, generalized, and unfocused.
When it becomes focused and when individuals come together to sustain
a campaign in support of a common social goal, we have a movement or
collective. Most of the time, it is more or less spontaneous and a dramatic
coming together of people whose relationships are not defined by rules
and procedures, but who instead share a common collective identity and
values or beliefs. During this cycle, huge followings can rise overnight
seemingly led by a charismatic champion. This cycle is typically brief and
brings challenges to convert the masses to a mobilized movement.

Focus -   Strengthen Networks
              Develop or support collective identity
              Legitimize group and promote movement culture
              Begin to define movement's vision and strategy

Hazards -   Change due to attacks (internal or external)
              Trying to win strategic objectives at this cycle
              People in it for themselves

Identity / Breakout - Most often, a charismatic champion that
launches a movement does not have the intent to mobilize the
masses to its strategic objectives. This cycle is most frequently
driven by the introduction of new champions, resources, and / or

new determination of the members. During this cycle, it is generally easier to gather an audience and new champions develop multiple strands. Unfortunately during this cycle, pseudo champions can arise as well with self-promotion, power, or ideals outside the collective identity in mind. It is also a danger at this cycle that a breakdown of the movement occurs or the strands will become too isolated. Ideally, as multiple strands do form during this cycle and co-evolve at different rates, the strongest survive and others co-mingle to develop later cycles. Where most movements get stuck in this phase or individuals lose interest, it is still critical to the overall development of the movement and it is during this cycle that generally defines the movements' identity. With this in mind and the numerous factors that may determine the evolution through this cycle, this could take years or even decades and for some create seemingly endless cycles where they repeat smaller cycles several times before progressing forward or achieving their objectives.

Focus -   Focus the energy and activism
            Develop and promote reference groups
            Identify and cultivate champions
            Clearly define strategic objectives
            Prepare and create strategies for opportunities

Hazards -   Tyranny of "Structurelessness"
            Unrealistic expectations or timeline
            Shotgun approach to activities
            Splinter groups may pop up
            Purists may resist change

Coalescence / Formalization - Some migratory or protest movements may be able to operate without formal or centralized organization, but most that desire to modify the society will in time come together in some form. This cycle usually converts excited masses from multiple strands into more disciplined membership and vague random actions into practical enterprise. During this cycle, resources are merged and a loose structure is created along with more formalized networks. Individuals and the movement begin to focus more long-term, and the members work towards more common goals. Most common catalyst for this cycle is the legitimization of the movement or group and power base beginning to change. The duration of this cycle can change widely-based on multiple factors and may be very short due to moving to next cycle or achieving strategic objectives, or prolonged due to shortage of resources and people resistant to the evolution to this cycle.

Focus -   Solidifying collective identity
               Structure and strategic focus to events
               Win Public Relations Battle
               People becoming independent social change agents
               Formalize the collective enterprise

Hazards -   Power becomes the group's new internal goals
               Infiltration or envelopment by larger organization
               Compromising with opposition for victory
               Lack of resources to create centralized organization
               Maintaining relative deprivation and / or loss of catalyst

Conclusions or consequences of a social movement: The conclusion of a social movement may not always be easily analyzed in terms of success or failure. It is clear, though, for those individuals involved in the movement, if active for any substantial time; things maybe previously taken for granted will never seem the same again, even after leaving the discipline of the movement and regardless of results.

Much like comparisons we have made to genetics and evolution, natural selection may play a role with the end result of particular strands or branches of a movement. As independent strands develop, the strongest will continue while others may die out or become extinct due to various factors such as suppression by the opposition, lack of necessary resources, or widespread apathy. As a whole, looking at the entire social movement, although strands may exist on and continue to evolve in different directions or spur spin off or splinter groups; if the movement continues on long enough it will ultimately meet perceived failure, accomplish an objective, or change forms and continue in a isolated or even larger targeted form.

Factorization - Can occur for multiple reasons and at any time in the life cycle of a movement, but will happen generally after a formalization of the movement takes place. This is generally due to power and the movement goals and focus then become more grounded in attainment of more power than the collective identity or values. On the other hand and almost completely contrary to this, a movement if prolonged in an identity cycle too long without a coalescing figure may also fracture in time as individuals and society do not take the movement seriously and it is unable to develop enough power to force any societal change.

Forced departure – As some movements transgress and become more and more radical simple civil disobedience may become uncivil. The consequences when champions or individuals acting of behalf of the reference group use measures outside of societal acceptance (such as violence) are that it generally destroys or forces the social movement's end.

Change thought - The goal and result here is personal transformation, bringing about social change by converting a majority of public opinion. It is then through an overwhelming consensus that it becomes imperative to implement their values. This in essence is changing the hearts and minds of the populace and generally requires the movement being legitimized along with large converts and membership.

Change policy - Success through societal manipulation, changing social institutions so that a program or policy may be implemented without regard to the number of people favoring the new policy or idea. In this form of success, relative numbers is less important and converts have less effect as much as a fundamental change in the social order.

Succession - This is less obvious in that the main thrust of the movement may apparently wither, but the remnants linger sometimes unseen and indefinitely as almost a cult. The new structure will be oriented more inwardly toward the gratifications that the individual members obtain from participation but make little serious effort any longer at significant social change.

Institutionalizing - The movement crystallizes into a formalized definite pattern, including traditions to uphold and possibly defend. The movement is generally legitimized in society and a percentage of its values are incorporated into the norm. Members feel themselves supporters of a worthy organization rather than campaigners in a sacrificial crusade. If properly created and strongly dependant on the members, this cycle may last almost indefinitely.

Final thoughts and analysis: By understanding the changes that can occur due to adaptive behaviors and evolution in genetics can reveal the critical elements needed to reconstruct parts of the body or genes that cause human genetic disorders. Similarly understanding the progression as well as natural and adaptive behaviors in social movements can reveal the critical elements to reconstruct parts or sustain its growth.

It was my findings and beliefs that the key to a successful Social Movement is the decentralized nature of the movement. Adaptation and natural selection is critical in the determinant of what actions work and which ones do not. The leaderless structure promotes creativity, power, resources, and knowledge be spread over the entire enterprise. It promotes the organic growth necessary for life and success. It is the group's and champion's responsibility to identify these strands that promote growth to the next cycles and become the liaison for the various branches to share and develop effectively.

Reference:

1987, "The Movement Action Plan, A Strategic Framework Describing the Eight Stages of Successful Social Movements", Bill Moyer

1998, "Diffusion Models of Cycles of protest as a Theory of Social Movements", Pamela E. Oliver & Daniel J. Myers (paper presented at the Congress of International Sociology Association, Montreal CAN)

1994-2009 Encyclopedia Britannica, Inc Lewis M. Killian, Ralph H. Turner, & Neil J. Smelser

2008, "The Starfish and the Spider: The Unstoppable Power of Leaderless Organizations", Ori Brafman & Rod A. Beckstorm

1952, "The Reformation of the Sixteeth Century", Roland Bainton

1930, "The Wesleyan Movement in the Industrial Revolution", Wellman Warner (Full text found online at Questia website: http://www.questia. com/PM.qst?a=o&d=6609690)

1975, "The Politics of Women's Liberation". Longman.

1993, "What is Promise Keepers? Men in Action", Ken Canfield

Promise Keepers Men of Integrity official website: http://www. promisekeepers.org/

1966, "The Civil Rights Movement: Momentum and Organization." Daedalus, Winter.

1999, "Waves of Protest: Social Movements Since the Sixties", Rowman & Littlefield

1997 – 2011, Culture Politics glossary of terms website: http:// culturalpolitics.net/social_movements/glossary

About the Authors

J. ERIC WILSON is the Executive Director for the Kentucky 9/12 Project, is on the advisory board for the National 9/12 Project, and sits as the chair for the national organization Constitutional Champions. He has been heavily involved in the 9/12 and Tea Party movements since their inception. He has appeared on the Glenn Beck show and been highlighted in articles in publications such as Financial Times, The Washington Post, Associated Press, Reuters, Wall Street Journal, and Focus on Family regarding the movements.

R. JUSTEN COLLINS is the Social Media Coordinator for the Kentucky 9/12 Project and serves on its executive board. He is a blogger and freelance writer whose colorful exploits have been published in assorted magazines for the past fifteen years. He was recently featured in a documentary following his personal journey to the Restoring Honor Rally in Washington, D.C.